LIVING
EUROPE

LIVING EUROPE

Exploring the Continent's Natural Boundaries

EDITOR:

NICK UPTON

B XTREE

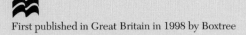

First published in Great Britain in 1998 by Boxtree

an imprint of Macmillan Publishers Ltd
25 Eccleston Place, London, SW1W 9NF
and Basingstoke

Associated companies throughout the world

ISBN 0 7522 1100 5

1 2 3 4 5 6 7 8 9 10

A CIP catalogue record for this book is available from the British Library.

Designed by DW Design
Colour origination by Speedscan Ltd, Basildon, Essex
Typeset by SX Composing, Rayleigh, Essex
Printed and bound in the UK by Bath Press Colour Books, Glasgow

Living Europe accompanies the television series of the same name
produced by Green Umbrella.

CONTENTS

ACKNOWLEDGEMENTS

This book is very much a team effort. Several members of the television production team (supported by two others who worked only on the book), have helped me tremendously by contributing all but two of the chapters, most of the 'boxes' on individual animals and the Introduction. I thank all of them for their hard work in producing the text, and for maintaining their enthusiasm for the project, despite tight deadlines and having to divide their time between working on the book and finishing the films.

The individual authors, whose initials appear after each piece of text, are:

AMY AITON
NIGEL ASHCROFT
ADAM CLARKE
JON CLAY
KATHRYN JEFFS
PETER JONES
RACHEL PINNOCK

In turn, all of us would like to thank the many, many people who helped us along the way in the making of this series. We could fill pages with the complete list of all the people, parks, universities and institutions who helped us, and credits do appear for many of them at the end of our films. Here, we would like to say a big thank you to everyone who has contributed in any way: by putting up with being endlessly quizzed on the telephone, by sending us information and ideas, by helping us in the field, by allowing us access to film in parks, ancient temples, private gardens and municipal sewers. At the end of the book all the authors have supplied a list of people whose ideas and information – or the help they provided on location – most inspired the text that they have produced. It is in no way meant to be a comprehensive list, and we apologise to anyone whose input appears to have been overlooked, but hope that this book and the *Living Europe* series do justice to the ideas and help that we were given.

NICK UPTON
Bristol, March 1998

For those who think that Europe is short of wildlife, this book should be a revelation. When I returned from Italy last year after a long trip directing sequences for the television series that inspired this book, I was often asked what we had filmed. By the time I had mentioned wolves, bears, wild boar and porcupines, I usually received a look of incredulity and a spluttered: 'What, in Italy?' One American even admitted that she thought we only had squirrels in Europe! She could not have been more wrong: lynx, bison, moose, reindeer, polar bears, walrus, whales and dolphins all live in Europe, not to mention a huge variety of birds, reptiles, insects and plants.

As a naturalist, some of the experiences I've had in Europe over the last two years match up to anything I've seen in South America, Africa or Asia on previous filming trips. I will always remember how small I felt when I saw my first bear in Italy's Abruzzo Mountains as we waited to film them by night camera, and the tingles that ran down my spine as wolves howled in the hills around. Snorkelling to within feet of a loggerhead turtle as it swam serenely through the blue waters off Greece was another great thrill, as was seeing huge griffon vultures drifting past at eye-level just 20m (66ft) away above the picturesque landscape of Extremadura in Spain.

The other thing that surprised many people was that nearly all the wildlife we filmed was within shouting distance of, or even in, villages or towns. We tend to assume that wildlife only lives in vast tracts of wilderness and in Europe, little (and some would argue no) wilderness remains; but this does not mean that there are no wild animals and plants. The land has often been managed for thousands of years, and wildlife has frequently found a way to live alongside, or even to take advantage of, our activities. Wildlife therefore often thrives in farmland and, increasingly, in cities.

In telling the story of Europe's wildlife on film, we sought to chronicle not just how animals have survived in fragments of wilderness, but also how many now depend on the 'humanized' land of the European continent, and how virtually all depend on the attitudes of local people for their survival. Along the way, we filmed and worked with some wonderful people: the olive harvesters on Crete who knew a use for nearly every plant on the hillsides around, and who served us with snail and spinach stew after we had filmed them at work; the Italian shepherds who had learned to live alongside the wolves and bears in the hills, and who plied us with wine and cheese; and the scientists we worked with, who shared and passed on their passion for porcupines, bears and chameleons.

This book is written by members of the television production team. Rather than seeking to produce a comprehensive treatise on the wildlife and nature reserves of Europe, we have sought to bring a flavour of our own personal experiences on location to the writing. Virtually all the places and creatures we describe here are those that we saw along the way, and many of them we filmed.

I hope that the impressions we leave are the ones we all gained: Europe remains a beautiful and varied continent, and it is still packed with wildlife. As is true around the world, some species are far rarer than they once were, and there is no cause for complacency. But the key to preserving what we have, and the health of Europe as a place to live, surely lies in seeking to understand the intimate links between people, land and wildlife.

Nick Upton
Bristol, March 1998

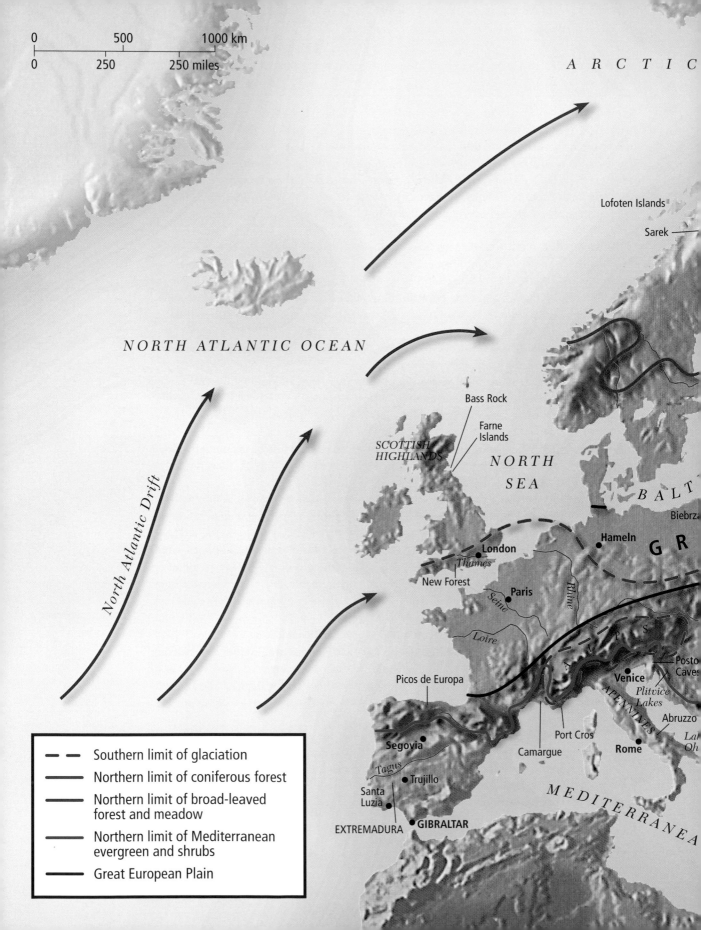

0   500   1000 km

0   250   250 miles

A R C T I C

Lofoten Islands

Sarek

NORTH ATLANTIC OCEAN

North Atlantic Drift

Bass Rock

Farne
Islands

*SCOTTISH
HIGHLANDS*

*N O R T H
S E A*

B A L T

Biebrza

Hameln

G R

London

Thames

New Forest

Seine

Paris

Rhine

Loire

S

Picos de Europa

Posto
Caves

Venice

*Plitvice
Lakes*

APENNINES

Abruzzo

Port Cros

Rome

*La
Oh*

Camargue

Segovia

Tagus

GIBRALTAR

Santa
Luzia

● Trujillo

EXTREMADURA

M E D I T E R R A N E A

Legend:

- – – – Southern limit of glaciation
- ——— Northern limit of coniferous forest
- ——— Northern limit of broad-leaved forest and meadow
- ——— Northern limit of Mediterranean evergreen and shrubs
- ━━━ Great European Plain

The great primeval forest of Bialowieza stretches across some 750sq km (300sq miles) of north-eastern Europe. Huge trees grow amid an unending tangle of rotting trunks and exposed roots. A single major road crosses the forest's dark expanse in an east–west direction, connecting Poland and its neighbour, Belarus. A few other roads come to an abrupt end deep in the forest in small villages where the local people still make a living from the forest. Along the border with Belarus, the forest has been cleared in a 12m (40ft) wide swathe to make room for an increasingly obsolete and rusty barbed-wire fence that stretches away into the distance. It is a stark reminder that even old political frontiers still rule the geographic map of Europe. But over the centuries man-made borders have come and gone while an underlying pattern of natural regions based on the soil, climate, altitude and terrain remained. Human settlement and farming was, and still is, largely based on this, as is the distribution of wildlife.

On both sides of the frontier the forest is now protected by new national laws, replacing the ancient forest laws that through past centuries preserved the area as a hunting reserve. The larger part of this wild forest, composed of oak, beech, lime and juniper, will be protected in recognition of its irreplaceable value as the most complete mixed lowland ancient woodland remaining in Europe.

If we go back 2,000 years to the start of the first millennium, the greater part of central lowland Europe was covered in dense forest of this kind, and occupied by the animals that epitomized wilderness: the wolf and the bear. To drive through this ancient and once impenetrable landscape today is to be reminded of the difference between what is truly wild and what has been tamed and settled by humans. Today, we can see that most of Europe is, in fact, a man-made landscape.

The transition from hunting and gathering to a more settled way of life, dependent on farming, started around 10,000 years ago with the domestication of animal livestock and the cultivation of primitive crops, notably cereals. Gradually the great forests, previously undisturbed, were cleared to allow for cultivation, and marshes were drained for pasture. The impact on wild creatures and plants, perhaps insignificant at first, often brought about permanent changes. These were not all deleterious, since cultivation that used traditional methods often made room for wild animals and plants, and even extended previously rare habitats. Nevertheless, as the process of settlement proceeded, man-made features were increasingly imposed on an underlying pattern of distinct natural regions, from the mighty mountain chains, such as the Alps, to the natural grasslands of the steppes. In addition, Europe's shores of steep cliffs, sandy Mediterranean beaches and rocky bays, pounded by wild Atlantic seas, were colonized by thousands of fishing settlements. Even the great marshes laced with running water, such as Biebrza, and the vast deltas and flood plains of rivers, such as the Danube, were peopled by farmers who utilized every local resource to create an economy.

The eastern boundary of Europe, for the purposes of this book, is the almost unbroken horizon of the Ukrainian steppes. This is the frontier across which invaders, both human and animal, came from Asia, and they appeared with regularity over thousands of years. To the north, our boundary lies beyond the Arctic Circle, where the edge of the permanent ice sheets, which constitute the kingdom of the polar bear and the walrus, forms another frontier. This is Europe's largest wilderness – an area that remains wild not because of protective laws but because it is one of the coldest, windiest and least inhabited places on the planet. It is a region that also takes us back in time to an Ice Age 20,000 years ago when glaciers covered Europe as far south as London, Paris, Hanover, Cracow and Kiev. Europe's million offshore islands are another great feature, from the small and isolated Bass Rock to islands as large as Crete and Sicily. Far out in the Atlantic, the Azores are the most westerly outpost. This geography of Europe suggests not so much a continent, but more a peninsular-like appendage to Asia that is separated to the south from its other neighbouring continent, Africa, by the Mediterranean Sea.

Some changes in Europe have come slowly. The extensive waving grasslands of the central plains flooded year after year until tamed just two centuries ago, and grazing, a form of farming developed long ago, preserved the ancient identity of fields and meadows that are medieval or even older in origin. Mountains and moors, colonized in some places thousands of years ago because of the security that their very inaccessibility offered, were also sometimes very slow to be permanently settled. A number of forests were preserved for hunting and the creation of great national parks has also succeeded in holding back the forces of change. In recent decades, however, with the rapid expansion of urban areas and the development of new forms of intensive farming, change has come all too quickly. But Europe is still home to over 200 kinds of mammal, and more than 500 species of bird, 130 species of reptile and amphibian, and countless insects and other invertebrates, which live among a fabulously diverse array of plants.

At the beginning of the 1990s the recognition that Europe has such valuable resources for wildlife and recreation was supported by important initiatives such as the formation of the Pan European Biological and Landscape Diversity Strategy prepared by the European Centre for Nature Conversation and the Council of Europe. Throughout Europe, scientists, naturalists and governments sought how to conserve and sustainably use Europe's most distinctive habitats: grassland, mountain, Arctic tundra, woodland, Mediterranean *maquis*, coast and wetland. The number of important nature areas for Europe runs to thousands and it is now up to every European nation to ensure that the best of them have some measure of protection, and that the wider countryside between them is effectively managed. This initiative, known as the Pan European Ecological Network, has been formed across all 54 countries of the region.

There is an increasing understanding of how wildlife uses European landscapes, both natural and man-made. In Europe the latter is certainly the most widespread and cannot be ignored for most, if not all, of Europe has been touched by the hands of humans. We do not need history books to see the work of countless generations of people who laboured to make a living from the land, for the evidence is there in the landscape. How wildlife has adapted to these changes is one of the most intriguing of all 'natural histories', and helps us to understand how European nature will survive into the twenty-first century.

The increasing political links between the countries of Europe means that for conservationists the map of the continent can now be redrawn along new lines that transcend national and political boundaries. This new map, featuring the great mountain ranges, the grasslands, the woods, the warm south and the frozen north, is a Europe as wildlife might perceive it. Within each of these landscapes on this 'new map of Europe', is a story to be told about how wildlife has coped alongside the rich human history of the region.

Today, on the brink of the twenty-first century, Europe means more than just a currency, a flag, an assembly and a judicature. In exploring the eight distinctive European habitats chapter by chapter, we can start to look at Europe as a rich and distinct patchwork of unique landscapes that has been created by successive waves of human civilization and which offers a wonderful diversity of wildlife.

PETER JONES
Bristol, March 1998

CHAPTER 1

THE CRADLE

BEGINNINGS: EARLY SETTLERS IN CRETE

Approaching the island of Crete by sea is a memorable experience; spectacularly rugged mountains, topped with snow for half the year, rise up impossibly steeply from the sparkling blue waters of the Mediterranean. If you're lucky, flying fish burst from the sea ahead of you to skim over the water, and playful dolphins ride your bow as you head for land. From afar, the scene has changed little for millennia but, as you get nearer, whitewashed houses, terraced slopes and walled harbours come into focus. This landscape has clearly been touched by humanity – but to what effect?

The bold limestone cliffs of the Dikti Mountains rise above woods of cypress, pine and oak. From the edge of the escarpment you can look out at a group of magnificent griffon vultures, or catch a glimpse of the rare bearded vulture, circling on thermals and looking down on the Lassithi plateau laid out like a map below. It is a shimmering patchwork of arable fields painted yellow by swathes of wild flowers, and fringed by orchards of almonds and apple trees glowing with spring blossom. The plain is encircled by ancient terraced slopes and crumbling stone walls, and echoes to the sounds of goat bells and singing woodlarks. It is a breathtakingly beautiful landscape, but one that is among the most humanized on earth, the product of over 400 generations of

Above
Crete's snow-topped Dikti Mountains provide a spectacular backdrop to the Lassithi plateau.

Opposite
The ancient Greek Temple of Poseidon, built 2,500 years ago, stands on a high cliff at Sounion, overlooking the Mediterranean sea.

Inset
Chameleons, brought to Europe from Africa centuries ago, live on Crete and at just a handful of other sites around the Mediterranean.

farmers and labourers. Here, the combined forces of nature and civilization have left their mark. Almost everywhere you look in Crete, a rich history is etched on the land revealing a fascinating glimpse of an earlier Europe, for it is on the island of Crete that human changes to the European landscape first began and here essential clues to much of Europe's wildlife heritage can be found.

Europe's warm southern lands, around the shores of the Mediterranean Sea, formed the 'cradle' of European civilization: the first region in Europe where human culture developed and spread. Human populations have grown rapidly in Europe over the last 8,000 years, fuelled by the efficiency that organized farming brought, and this expansion began around the Mediterranean. The advance of human civilization in Europe, accompanied by the clearance of land for agriculture and by the establishment of cities, is the single factor that has had the greatest impact on the way Europe looks today, since the end of the last Ice Age around 12–13,000 years ago. The way that wildlife has adapted to humanized landscapes and has found a way to live alongside us with varying degrees of success is a story that needs to be told, since the future health and appearance of European landscapes depends on our understanding of the links between nature and land management. Moreover, our own health and well-being, as is increasingly becoming all too apparent, is also inextricably linked with that of our environment.

The story begins on the island of Crete, whose landscape was transformed by the first great European civilization, the Minoan. The first permanent settlers, and ancestors of the Minoans, came to Crete some 8,000 years ago from Asia, most probably from the area now known as Turkey, where the remains of Catal Huyuk, which dates from around 8,500 years ago and is thus one of the earliest known large towns, survive in the east of Turkey. Catal Huyuk was home to some 6,000 people, who clearly worshipped the wild bulls or aurochs that roamed the area, for the huge horns of these great beasts adorned many shrines and dwellings. The people of Catal Huyuk obviously hunted the aurochs, but it is not certain whether they were yet herding a domesticated form of them as cattle. Archaeological remains do, however, confirm that domesticated sheep and goats, descended from larger wild sheep and goats, were herded around Catal Huyuk, and the reliable supply of food that domestic animals gave this culture may partly explain how such a large human settlement was possible. Of even greater importance, though, may have been the crops of wheat and barley which they grew. The origins of this agriculture, along with those of domesticated animals, lay further to the east in the Fertile Crescent of the region we now call the Middle East.

The earliest evidence of agriculture in the world comes from the remains of a 10,000-year-old farming village that has been excavated beneath the ancient city of Jericho, on the west bank of the River Jordan, in what is now Israeli-occupied Jordan. The Fertile Crescent was a broad arching sweep of natural grasslands and open oak and pistachio woodlands, and included what is now northern Israel and the Lebanon, the more fertile regions of northern Syria and the valleys of the Tigris and Euphrates rivers in Iraq. It was in this region that naturally growing wild emmer wheat and einkorn wheat, along with wild barley, were first domesticated. Seeds from stands of these plants had probably been collected and eaten here since the end of the last Ice Age, by people from a variety of hunter–gatherer societies, who relied on wild plants and animals for their survival. Around 10,000 years ago, it seems that they began to collect grains from the wild grasses and grew the world's first crops. Particular features of these grasses, such as large, long-lasting seed heads, which allowed easy harvesting, were selectively bred over the next 2,000 years, and the first domesticated strains of wheat and barley were born, along with some domesticated legumes, such as lentils, chickpeas and peas, again descended from wild forms. Cattle, sheep, goats and pigs were also domesticated from their wild ancestors in this region during the same period, a time of remarkable transformation in the way people lived.

Ever since then, the future look of Europe was set to change; people, reliably fed by crops of cereals and legumes, along with milk and meat from herds of domestic animals (which also provided leather for clothing and new means of transport) rapidly increased in numbers and began to spread. The Fertile Crescent was bounded by high mountains to the east, and by deserts to the south, but to the west lay Europe and the fertile fringes of the Mediterranean Sea. It was in this direction that the major movement of agricultural peoples originating in the Fertile Crescent took place; they created cities and cleared land for grazing their animals and growing their crops as they went.

Agriculture has spread throughout virtually the whole of Europe over the last 8,000 years. It has largely replaced the former type of existence that relied on hunting wild animals on the plains and in the forests of Europe and collecting plants for food. This way of life was practised by people living in far lower densities throughout the continent prior to the advance of civilization; sustained by efficient agriculture, a hundred times as many people can be supported by the same area of land as is possible through hunter–gathering. The combined effects of agriculture and of far higher densities of people on the landscape and on wildlife are potentially immense, but what in fact were they?

The first major impact in Europe of this new agricultural way of life was felt in the Mediterranean region, and the clearest evidence for these changes has been found on the island of Crete. Settlers came to Crete and other Mediterranean islands, such as Cyprus and the Cyclades, around 8,000 years ago. They brought cereals with them, along with sheep, cattle and goats, and began to prosper. Animal bones found in ancient caves, show that a now extinct fauna of grazing animals once populated Crete, an island which, 22,000 years ago, was home to at least seven species of deer, ranging in size from that of a dog to larger than a red deer stag; a pig-sized, mountain-living hippopotamus; and a bullock-sized elephant, along with giant insectivores and rodents. No remains of large predators have been found on Crete, and the ancient deer and other mammals may well have had poorly developed escape reactions. Some, or even all of them, may have died out due to natural climatic changes on Crete, but the last of them seem to have disappeared about 12,000 years ago, around the time that hunting and fishing people would have been capable of reaching the island by sea. It is possible that some of the native mammals may have been hunted to extinction. Since then domestic grazers have had the island's vegetation largely to themselves.

During the 3,000 years after their arrival, the agricultural settlers of the Mediterranean islands also began to cultivate olives and grapes, which seem to have been domesticated and selectively bred from wild olives and wild vines. The earliest clear signs of olive oil and wine being consumed come from traces in jugs and cups found at an excavated grave site, dated to around 5,000 years ago, on the island of Naxos in the Cyclades. But it was on the far larger island of Crete, which is some 260km (156 miles) long and varies between 12 and 60km (7 to 36 miles) wide, that the descendants of the early settlers created the Minoan civilization, which lasted from around 4,600 to 3,100 years ago. Ruins of dozens of Minoan towns and palaces have been discovered and many impressive burial sites with narrow 'slit tombs' carved into solid rock have been unearthed, so much about the Minoan way of life has now been revealed.

The relics the Minoans left hint at a culture that was influenced and inspired by the wildlife around them. Their ornate burial casks were often painted with intricate images of wildlife: spiders, scorpions, deer, lilies and sea daffodils were depicted, while their greatest

Left

Tree frogs gather by the thousand at a Cretan lake created by potters who have dug for clay here since Minoan times.

Opposite

The dramatic Gorge of Ha in western Crete, where golden eagles and choughs often circle above the ancient scree slopes.

palace, at Knossos, was adorned with beautiful frescoes of dolphins and octopuses. Their civilization was built on a firm agricultural basis, and the Minoans grew rich by trading olive oil, wine and wheat to less developed societies around the shores of the Mediterranean. Extensive storerooms filled with giant pots for storing wine and olive oil can still be seen at the palaces of Knossos and Phaistos. In return for their agricultural produce, the Minoan traders often sought tin, which was needed to turn copper into bronze, a strong and highly prized metal with which they used to make weapons and ornaments.

Almost everything on Crete seems touched by the human hand, and links between the past and the present abound in today's landscape and in the way many people still live. A small lake near the village of Thrapsano has a connection with continuous human activity going back thousands of years. This region, renowned for its fine clays, is thought to have been the centre of pot-making in Minoan times, and the name Thrapsano actually means 'shard'. The tradition of making giant storage pots is still strong here, and several large potteries, which export their wares around the world, survive to this day. The lake was formed long ago by potters gathering clay, as they still do today. The resulting depression is now filled with fresh water and, being the only significant stretch for miles around, has become a true wildlife hotspot. In the spring, migrant swallows, martins, egrets, glossy ibises, stilts, ruff and other waders visit to rest and feed on their passage north to Europe from Africa, while stripe-necked terrapins bask on the shores. Since the wildlife riches of this human-made site have been recognized, the lake has become a fixture in the itinerary of many visiting naturalists. The local community, too, has taken increasing interest in it, and a ban on hunting, which is enforced rigorously, was recently imposed. The lake has also just been extended, and islands created, to make it even more attractive to the migrants and to attract winter wildfowl such as shoveler and garganey ducks and black-necked grebes. This is just one of an encouraging number of conservation schemes that are being created on Crete, aimed at preserving the diverse communities of wildlife that have developed over the millennia alongside traditional human use of the landscape.

In the spring, the air around the lake begins to pulsate with a raucous dusk chorus of green toads, marsh frogs and tree frogs which have travelled to this spot from the surrounding olive groves and vineyards to breed. As the amphibian chorus builds, scorpions and geckos creep out from their daytime hiding places to hunt for insects, and edible dormice emerge from tree holes in the olive groves to search for food. In the limestone hills above the lake, hordes of snails emerge in the cool of night to graze on vegetation. They are considered a great delicacy throughout Crete, and are much sought after by human collectors, but the snails have voracious natural predators too. Cretan spiny mice live among the stones of ancient olive or vine terraces, and on goat-grazed rocky slopes. These little-known mammals, found elsewhere only in Egypt and Israel and possibly Cyprus, live in small colonies dominated by single females. They hop around hyperactively in search of snails, which they grasp with sharp teeth, before chiselling the shell away in a spiral pattern to reach the soft flesh beneath. The location of their burrows, usually in crevices under or within limestone boulders, is given away by numerous, telltale mounds of discarded snail shells.

With the exception of the ancient mammal fauna that disappeared before the advent of agriculture, Crete's wildlife seems to have survived intact since then. Moreover, the island's age-old farming practices have given the wildlife plenty of time to adapt to the changes brought about by a human presence on the landscape, and even to take advantage of them. In early spring, the olive groves become a riot of colour as carpets of flowers spread across the ground, attracting the first butterflies and beetles of the season to compete for nectar with the bees which have been cultured here for thousands of years. As the olives ripen, their owners come to knock the olives down into nets with long sticks, in a way that has not changed for over 2,000 years. Scenes of men beating olive trees with long staves and picking up the olives from sheets spread below were depicted on vases dating back 2,500 years. An ancient olive tree itself, with its twisted, gnarled trunk, and its flat crown shaped by centuries of pruning to ensure it could be reached for harvesting, is the very image of continuity. Some individual trees have been shown to be more than 2,000 years old by counting the annual growth rings in boughs that have been cut off. The growing of olives is still lucrative on Crete, since there is a huge world market for high-quality olives and olive oil, and olive groves are currently on the increase on the island. Olive harvesting remains a typical festive family event, for this is still a laborious task even where an elegantly simple, hand-held mechanical device now complements the old staves.

Nothing in Crete's agricultural land is left untouched by humans and yet insects, birds and lizards find vineyards happy hunting grounds. Every olive grove is a small reserve where the cicadas sing ceaselessly, geckos scuttle in and out of holes in the tree-trunks, and woodchat shrikes impale their insect prey on thorn bushes – and these days on barbed wire, too – along with the odd lizard and small bird, in order to create their gruesome 'larders' of stored food.

Alongside Crete's many olive groves and vineyards grow large areas of scrubby, relict woodland known as *maquis*, a classic Mediterranean form of vegetation composed of shrubs and stunted woody plants that are prevented from growing into large trees by grazing. Lower-growing Mediterranean vegetation with scrubby plants only, and no large bushes or trees, is generally known as *garigue*, but is called *phrygana* on Crete. Goats have played a crucial role in shaping the look of this landscape since their introduction to the island 8,000 years ago, and some of the spiny bushes take on weird abstract shapes as a result of their browsing. Today, many of the domestic goats graze rocky, largely inaccessible regions where they are difficult to herd, and they appear to be very shy and rather wild. It seems that some of the first domestic goats introduced to Crete became completely wild. The descendants of these runaways, the famous wild goats, or kri-kri, have reverted to an ancestral form rather like alpine ibex, and now roam wild on Crete's high White Mountains (see box, p. 19: 'The Cretan Wild Goat').

The Cretan Wild Goat

The view from the top of the Samaria gorge in southern Crete is wonderful: one of the vast limestone cliffs of the White Mountains faces you, rising vertically above cypresses, prickly oaks and pines. A winding path takes you steeply down through 15km (9 miles) of spectacular scenery, with sheer cliffs hemming you in on both sides as you approach the sea. If you scan the tree-covered hillside facing you, you may be rewarded with a glimpse of the famous Cretan wild goats, otherwise known as *agrímis* or kri-kris. They have thick buff-coloured fur, and the powerful males have huge curved horns up to a metre in length (very like Alpine ibex) and long, shaggy beards.

The ancestors of these dramatic animals are thought to have been domesticated goats brought by the first human settlers to Greece about 8,000 years ago. Some ran free in Crete's inaccessible mountains, and have reverted over the millennia to a wild, ibex-like form. The males battle with each other, violently clashing heads together, to gain dominant positions within the herds.

These large, but surprisingly agile, creatures became symbolic for Crete; they appear on Minoan seals and vessels, and they have inspired numerous place names around the island, such as Agrimokephala ('wild goat head') Mountain. The *agrími*'s longevity and enduring presence in Cretan life is also apparent from the number of folk tales surrounding its befriending of shepherds.

The *agrími* was once found in all Crete's high terrain, but hunting with rifles restricted it to the White Mountains. Protection of the *agrími* became the first objective of modern conservation on Crete in the 1920s when the Samaria Gorge National Park was set up. Small populations were also moved to three islet reserves off Crete's north coast. Their numbers have since increased in the White Mountains; some have become used to the hordes of tourists who walk through the gorge in the summer, and have become quite tame. Large herds now roam the islands (one of which is easily visited by boat from Aghios Nikolaos), but their presence here is controversial, since this is not ideal habitat for goats. Water and plant food are restricted, and both have to be supplemented. The goats have also been grazing one of the world's rarest plants which only grows on Crete. There are plans to reintroduce the goats into a more suitable habitat, which includes a colony of griffon vultures, in a proposed new reserve near Neápolis in the north of Crete.

The word *agrími* derives from the Greek, and means simply 'animal' or 'beast', but to most Cretans the goats are known as kri-kris, a name with an unusual history. It comes from when the Cretan government presented the US President Truman with one as a gift. It was taken to Washington State Zoo where schoolchildren named the goat 'kri-kri' (literally 'cre-cre' from 'Crete-Crete', in the same way that the giant panda at London Zoo was named Chi-Chi after 'China').

KJ/AC/NU

It has been suggested, since the time of Plato over 2,300 years ago, that Crete, and the Mediterranean in general, is a 'lost Eden' – a land that was covered with magnificent forests before the advance of agriculture, and which men first cleared with axes and then turned into a relative desert by overgrazing. However, recent botanical investigations suggest that this pervasive 'ruined landscape' theory is somewhat misleading and unnecessarily negative. It seems to have been based partly on inaccurate translations of old Greek and Latin texts: the ancient writers may have unwittingly exaggerated the effects of deforestation, since they may not have realized how forests can regenerate. The theory also tends to overlook the natural

Above

*A preying mantis
snatches a cicada in a
Greek olive grove.*

processes of erosion in the Mediterranean region. Crete's rugged scree slopes, such as those around the spectacular gorge of Ha in western Crete, above which golden eagles and choughs are frequently seen, may look today much as they would have done in Minoan times. The bare look is easily explained by aeons of frost-shattering and violent winter storms eroding the steep mountain slopes, without blaming the grazing of goats.

The landscape of Crete has undoubtedly become more open over time as woodland was cleared for fuel, building materials and to make way for agriculture, and grazing does create more open scrub and maintains it that way. Many plants, however, benefit from this openness; Crete, far from being a lost Eden, is fabulously rich in wild flowers, with some 2,000 known species, a tenth of which grow nowhere else. Its richness is largely overlooked by visitors, most of whom come in the hot summer months when the island's scrubby *maquis* and *phrygana* can seem dry and dead, but in spring these produce a riot of colour as they flower, with whole hillsides turning cherry red with Cretan ebony and oleander, studded with yellow spikes of asphodels and blue bushes of rosemary. Limestone outcrops are the Meccas for visiting botanists, as they support the widest array of plants, including a host of colourful butterfly, bee and spider orchids.

Crete's multitude of flowers encourage a wide array of insects, including a host of attractive butterflies, and the insects in turn support many insectivorous birds and lizards, such as the attractive ocellated skink or *liakoni*. Like all skinks, it has tiny legs and moves rather like a snake, and can be seen basking on rocks or stalking insects. Although harmless to humans, many Cretans are terrified of it and have a saying: 'If the *liakoni* bites you with its mouth, call a doctor, but if it stings you with its tail, call the priest.'

Crete's plants survive so well, despite the grazing of goats, most probably because they became adapted to grazing by the indigenous island fauna of deer, dwarf hippopotamus and elephants, long before goats arrived. The incredible spikiness of many Cretan plants, along with an array of oils and resins – which makes walking on Crete a painful, if aromatic experience – almost certainly evolved as a defence against this long extinct browsing fauna. Even some of the most delicate plants survive in heavily grazed areas, nestling between the thorns of the tougher plants. Crete also has many rocky ledges and slopes inaccessible to even the most agile goat, where rare endemic species can still survive.

Paradoxically, many of the oils and resins which provide protection against grazers have led to plants, such as rosemary, thyme, oregano and sage, being prized as herbs or for use in healing teas. A huge range of 'weed' plants, or *horta*, are also collected by people from all walks of life on Crete. This custom and many other surviving local traditions on Crete, reflect an ancient and intimate understanding of wild flowers and the natural world generally. Such interest and feeling for nature, however, was taken to new heights by the classical Greek civilization that arose on the mainland some 2,500 years ago, based on the same agricultural triad of wheat, olives and wine, supported by the grazing of goats.

Above

An ocellated skink, much feared in Cretan folklore, basks on the walls of a Minoan palace.

The Minoan ascendancy of the Mediterranean came to an end around 3,500 years ago, when the Myceneans, whose power base was the great southern peninsula of Greece, the Peloponnese, took over control of Crete. Some theories suggest that many of the Minoan palaces were destroyed by a tidal wave caused by a huge volcanic eruption around that time on the island of Santorini, 120km (72 miles) north of Crete, and by subsequent earthquakes. A huge fire at Knossos in 1380 BC finally destroyed the partially rebuilt palace about a hundred years later. The Myceneans had been slowly building up a powerful civilization on the Peloponnese since around 4,000 years ago, based on the same farming practices that had served Crete so well, but their power declined rapidly within some 900 years. Mystery still surrounds their decline, and little is known of their impact on the wildlife of the region, but one theory is that a prolonged cooling of the climate may have ruined their vital agricultural base, and a period known as the Greek Dark Ages began about 1100 BC, which lasted for roughly 300 years until the rise of classical Greece began.

The ancient Greeks respected and revered natural beauty. Their greatest monuments were always built in the most beautiful natural settings they could find, where they felt that their gods, spiritual embodiments of the forces of nature, would be most likely to live. The fabulous Temple of Poseidon, who was the Greek god of the sea, dominates the clifftops at Sounion on the southernmost headland of Attica, just south of Athens. Commanding an impressive view over the blue waters of the Aegean, the temple, which dates from the fifth century BC, is a haven for wild flowers, and every crevice in the rocky headland sprouts colourful blooms of campions and thistles in spring. Alpine swifts nest in the cliffs below, and frequently whip through the white marble columns of the temple in their pursuit of insects. In spring and autumn, the headland is also a great vantage point for spotting flocks of migrant shearwaters, egrets, herons and raptors flying by, while the scrubby bushes all around provide resting places for smaller birds. The temple almost certainly acted as a vital navigational landmark for sailors. Since the rugged, mountainous countryside of ancient Greece was so hard to traverse by land, the sea became an increasingly important way of travelling from one city to another and for conducting trade, and the majority of cities at that time were built close to the shores of the Mediterranean.

Much of the coast of Attica today has been developed, but even the tiniest pocket of open land becomes a riot of flowering Jerusalem sage, broom, rock roses and other shrubs in the spring. Perhaps the most enchanting spot is a little limestone peninsula at Schinias, near Marathon. This was the site of the famous battle from which, according to legend, the messenger Pheidippides ran 42km (26 miles) back to Athens to announce victory over the Persians, dropping dead soon afterwards. His efforts supposedly inspired the long-distance marathon race. On this undeveloped rocky spur of land at Schinias, tiny open glades studded with anemones, fritillaries, orchids and violets break up the spiky tangle of pink-flowering wild almond bushes and swathes of yellow spurges. The flowering bushes are temporary havens for many migrant warblers, flycatchers and shrikes, some of which stay to breed in the summer, and the humid air created by the sea crashing against the rocks below keeps this little jewel of the Attican coast green and vibrant with life long after much of Greece has become dry and parched.

Perhaps the most spectacular classical site of all, which was developed over a long period in the fifth and sixth centuries BC, although it had been a simple shrine before this, lies 150km (90 miles) to the north-west at Delphi. The great Temple of Apollo was famed for its oracle, and people came from all over Greece to receive largely indecipherable riddles concerning their future from the Pythia or priestess. Delphi's fine stadium, amphitheatre, and many temples, shrines and treasuries are spread out over a steeply descending hillside that affords a sweeping view down an olive-clad valley towards the sea. The whole site is hemmed in by spectacular cliffs (known as the 'shining rocks') rearing up behind, which are mere foothills to the soaring Mount Parnassus above.

In the spring, the clear mountain air at Delphi reverberates to the sweet trillings of rock nuthatches singing among the ruins. Perching on the ancient columns, they throw back their heads with an abandoned air and proclaim their territorial ownership with incredible power. They build remarkable nests in any suitable crevices, often the gaps between the giant building blocks of temples, using up to 40kg (88lb) of mud to line the nest and to build a bulging tunnel-like entrance, artfully camouflaged with berries, beetle wings and caterpillars hammered into place. They flit among the ruins gathering insects to feed their young, waiting for breaks in the stream of visiting tourists before swooping across the paths to enter their rarely noticed nests. Their trillings are complemented by sweet snatches of song from iridescent blue rock thrushes which perch momentarily on the roofs of the temples before darting off to catch large insects visiting the site's many flowers. High above the temples, golden eagles cruise along the clifftops, peregrine falcons and kestrels noisily dispute the best breeding ledges, and squadrons of warbling alpine choughs tumble, roll and swoop down from above, sometimes perching on the highest columns before heading down to the valley below.

Delphi was considered to be the centre of the universe in ancient Greece, and there is even a circular marble 'navel' stone at Delphi that marks the precise central point. In many ways, this view was not far wrong; Greece was undoubtedly the cultural centre of the world for several centuries, and much of the world's thinking and civilization has been influenced by the ancient Greeks ever since. An incredible revolution in philosophy, science and art took place in Greece between 700 and 200 BC. Much of the early thinking was clearly inspired by the natural beauty that surrounded them, and many of the great Greek writers like Homer, Euripides and Theocritus glorified nature in their writing. Aristotle, Plato's most famous pupil, was the first to try and make sense of the fabulous profusion and diversity of nature. He began to classify mammals, birds, reptiles and insects into distinct groups and to try to name as many kinds as he could. The system he devised, with later modifications by Linnaeus, survives today. By actually studying nature, rather than relying on philosophical theory alone, the Greek natural philosophers developed the first concepts of how plants and animals depend on one another, how predators and prey interact and even how only those creatures whose structure suited their place in nature would survive, a rudimentary version of the concept of natural selection. They also looked for links between the behaviour of wildlife and human activities: Democritus believed many advances in civilization were the result of observing animal habits. He thought human weaving was inspired by spiders spinning webs, singing by bird song, and that our use of clay in house building was influenced by watching swallows constructing nests from mud. Hippocrates, the founder of Greek medicine and of the medical ethics to which today's doctors still adhere, based many cures on an intimate understanding of botany and herbal remedies.

The ancient Greeks were also the first to raise competitive sport to cult status. Their huge athletics stadium at Olympia in the western Peloponnese survives remarkably intact. Quadrennial athletic contests between the Greek city-states were held here for a thousand years until AD 393, and were the inspiration for the modern Olympic games. An arched entrance-way leads into the grass-banked stadium, and the start and finish lines for sprint races, 180m (600ft) apart, are clearly preserved, along with paved areas for the judges. The sporting events here were originally imbued with great religious significance, and they were held in

honour of the most powerful god, Zeus. An extensive 'sacred grove' of trees was sited right next to the stadium, within which several temples, altars and shrines were built. Such groves were preserved for the gods, whom the Greeks believed would choose to walk here, or appear in the form of animals and birds. Olympia is still surrounded by rich woodland, and the site itself is interspersed with many large, shade-giving oaks, poplars, pines and wild olives. The vibrant pink blossoms of Olympia's many Judas trees attract hordes of bees, and wild flowers grow rampantly among the fallen columns of ancient temples. The air is filled in spring with the ringing songs of serins and the melodies of warblers. Blackcaps feed on fallen wild olives, stonechats hop among the ancient altars hunting for insects, and plunder beakfuls of flying termites as they pour out into the warm sunshine from nests in the ground. The stonechats compete with hordes of colourful Peloponnese wall lizards for this bumper crop of food.

Serins and collared flycatchers peck away at the shell-limestone walls of the treasuries, gathering the calcium they need for their developing eggs. Montpelier snakes, up to 2m (6ft 6in) long, live between the stones of later Byzantine ruins in a quieter corner of the site, hunting for lizards and rodents, which they subdue with poison fangs. Despite their venom, these shy creatures are of no real danger to humans, as only swallowed prey is exposed to the poison fangs far back in their mouths. Around the perimeter of the site lies an extensive series of badger setts, and a trained eye can spot badger trails and minor excavations for insects and worms throughout the site. Badger footprints can even be found in the sands of the ancient running track within the stadium after a damp night, but the animals are usually hidden away below ground long before the sun is up.

In the hills above the Olympic stadium where grunts of athletic endeavour once filled the air, flower-filled meadows are the scene for animal contests of equal intensity, if not speed. Male spur-thighed tortoises repeatedly ram one another in trials of strength, trying to topple opponents on to their backs to establish dominance, before trundling through the undergrowth after females in the race to secure a mate. A male will overtake his intended, head-butt her to a standstill and nibble at her head and tail in a less than gentle way, before climbing aboard and emitting a series of high pitched moans, in time with sticking out a pink fleshy tongue, as he attempts to mate with her. The female remains extremely nonchalant, often continuing to munch flowers and green leaves as a male mounts her – the male frequently toppling off in his excitement. Greece is also home to the very similar Hermann's tortoise, which lacks horny spurs on its back legs, and to the larger marginated tortoise, which can be over 30cm (1ft) long. Greek tortoises were once heavily collected for the pet trade, but this practice is now banned, and their populations have recovered well throughout the country. They are quite often seen crossing roads, a bad habit that creates a major hazard for themselves and vehicles alike.

The landscape of central and northern Greece is much greener, cooler and more wooded than the south, and some of the landscapes are quite unforgettable. At Metéora, vast pillars of hard conglomerate rock tower up to 400m (1,280ft) above the plain of Thessaly below, where softer sedimentary rock has been eroded away over the millennia. Egyptian vultures nest on ledges on these phenomenal rocks, and soar alongside screaming parties of swifts and flitting red-rumped swallows. But the rocks have long been home to more than wildlife; Christian hermits sought solitude and closeness to God atop the rocks as far back as the tenth century, while an organized monastic community developed here from the eleventh century, reaching its greatest extent in the sixteenth century with thirteen monasteries and about twenty smaller settlements perched on the rocks. The monks came and went from them on precarious wooden ladders, or in baskets hauled up the rock faces. The monks once found refuge from a series of invaders from the north, and could pray to God and commune with nature in peace and solitude. Six of these remarkable monasteries, founded about 600 years ago and built in an elaborate Byzantine style, have survived, but today's monks and nuns seem to have little peace, as the many bridges and steps cut into the rock provide easy access to streams of visiting tourists.

The tree-clad Pindos Mountains, which form a snow-capped backdrop to Metéora for much of the year, make up Greece's mountainous spine, running right up to the border with Albania. Many of their lower slopes are covered with fruit, almond and chestnut trees, but higher up grow thick forests of beech, oak and pine. These forests are still home to wolves and golden jackals. Both these canines are found throughout central and northern Greece, although they are heard far more than they are seen, as they are much persecuted. Bears, and a few lynx too, live in the northern Pindos, and even lions roamed Greece until as recently as the fourth century BC, especially around Mount Olympus, the legendary abode of the gods. Such lions spawned the legends of Androcles pulling a thorn from a lion's paw, and of Herakles (Hercules) slaying the Nemean lion. The disappearance of lions from Greece, and the reduced ranges of wolves and jackals, no doubt reflect the clearance of many forests in Greece as agriculture and grazing increased, but the rise of the next great Mediterranean civilization further to the west, that of the ancient Romans, may have been a contributing factor.

Just as the military power of Greece declined, partly through warring between its city-states, the city of Rome in Italy, which had been founded in 753 BC, was rapidly growing in strength. In a period of just fifty years or so, between 220 and 167 BC, the Romans took over the Greek colonies in Sicily and Italy, moved rapidly to control mainland Greece and brought almost the whole of the inhabited world within their rule. They stamped their imprint on landscapes and on political and cultural life wherever they went. Again, wheat, wine and olives were the agricultural mainstay for the Romans, and they brought a new level of order and efficiency to agriculture.

Rome was supposedly founded by Romulus who, according to legend, was raised and suckled, along with his brother Remus, by a she-wolf. A famous bronze statue depicts this maternal scene, and replicas of it appear all over Rome. The early Romans, like the ancient Greeks, invested animals and wild places with spiritual powers. But although they recognized similarities between their senior deities, which included Jupiter, Juno and Venus, and the Greeks deities such as Zeus, Hera and Aphrodite, the Romans related many of their gods and goddesses with the concerns of daily, and especially agricultural, life. These utilitarian deities had to be provided with ritual offerings, and in return were expected to promote fertility (Ceres), to protect against crop disease (Robigus), and to aid such practical details as harrowing (Imporcitor), sowing (Insitor) and even manuring (Sterculius). If the Romans had had bicycles, they would undoubtedly have had a goddess Punctura!

The increasingly practical ancient Romans believed that nature was there to be exploited by them. While the ancient Greeks preserved areas solely for their spiritual value, the Romans were far more concerned with their economic potential. They were very effective farmers in many ways, working their fertile lands intensively, and came to equate utility with beauty. They cherished neat, ordered landscapes which, in their eyes, they had improved by taming the wilderness, seen as the 'haunt of beasts' and a 'barren waste'. By controlling landscapes, they were able to make up for what they saw as the deficiencies of nature. The impressively regimented vine terraces that march along some 8km (5 miles) of rugged coastline in the Cinque Terre region of north-west Italy typify their approach to the land. Their way of dividing land up into a geometric chequerboard of squares, known as 'centuriation', along with their bullet-straight roads, again characterized their approach to land use. They were also the first masters of irrigation, building extensive aqueducts to carry water where it was needed, and even draining vast mountain lakes to provide both water for irrigation and new land for cultivation.

The population and wealth of the Roman Empire grew rapidly as it expanded, and the city of Rome became filled with great monuments to celebrate victories. Wide avenues with huge, ornate archways were also built to accommodate parades of victorious armies returning with the spoils of war. The Colosseum at Rome is perhaps the most impressive surviving monument, but this great amphitheatre has a dark and bloody history. Built between AD 72 and 80 to provide entertainment for the increasingly decadent people of Rome, it was the scene of mass slaughter. The Romans developed a great taste for watching contests between human opponents, gladiators and wild animals, and between increasingly unlikely combinations of animals. To feed this hunger for novel forms of bloodshed, huge numbers of large animals were brought from all over their empire, including local wolves and bears, African elephants, ostriches, lions, leopards, crocodiles and Asian tigers. Nero even managed to stage a show featuring polar bears catching seals. The numbers of animals brought to the

Colosseum to be slaughtered, or as the Romans termed it, 'to be hunted', was phenomenal: 9,000 animals were killed in a hundred days at the Colosseum when it was first dedicated, and over 11,000 were slaughtered on another occasion to celebrate Trajan's conquest of Dacia. Few Romans saw anything wrong in this 'sport', but the great orator, essayist and politician Cicero, to his credit, did protest against the slaughter of elephants, which he considered to be almost human.

The Romans' ability to catch and transport so many large, live wild animals from far-flung corners of their empire to Rome is actually very impressive, considering they had no access to modern dart-gun technology. They must have had a deep understanding of wildlife, but their use of such knowledge as a means to control and subdue animals was typical of their approach to nature. The Romans justified these collecting expeditions as a way of removing danger from people and agriculture. The impact of such large-scale collecting, combined with an insatiable appetite for hunting, was to drive many large animals to extinction around their empire, and many of the larger mammals in Italy were heavily reduced in numbers as well. Today, there is little to remind us of the Colosseum's original use. Kestrels nest high in its walls, and cats, descendants of creatures brought over from Egypt, live among its arches. Italian and common wall lizards scuttle over the stones, and armies of harvester ants carry grass seeds back to their nests over the very cobblestones where Roman soldiers once marched past the Colosseum bearing the spoils of war.

PRESENT-DAY FAUNA IN ITALY

Despite the depredations of the ancient Romans, and the extensive activities of hunters throughout the country ever since, Italy still supports a rich and varied fauna, especially where traditional land uses have survived. The spectacular Abruzzo Apennines for example, although less than a two-hour drive from Rome, are home to both wolves and bears, along with chamois (see boxes, p. 30: 'Italian Bears' and p. 53: 'The European Grey Wolf'). The key to the survival of these animals lies partly in the establishment of an extensive national park, founded in 1922, which now encompasses a number of villages and much agricultural and pastoral land, but it also reflects the traditional 'live and let live' attitude of local shepherds towards wolves and bears. Sheep have been grazed in the Abruzzo region since before the era of ancient Rome, and the shepherds here have always lived alongside wolves. Over time, they found ways to protect their flocks, always bringing them into walled enclosures at night or when the weather closed in. They also raised large white dogs, which acted as vigilant guards and defenders, alongside the sheep. In the past, they did kill the occasional wolf that consistently found ways to dodge their defences, but they never set out to persecute or exterminate wolves in the area. Indeed, the shepherds came to respect the wolf for its intelligence and bravery, and they have continued to herd sheep alongside a population of wolves in this way. Today, they would never seek to kill the wolves, not just because they are protected by law, but because the Abruzzo wolves have become less of a threat to their flocks. The wolves were once driven to prey on domestic animals here, since hunters had managed to kill much of the wolves' natural prey, including all the red and roe deer in the area. But now that the park has successfully reintroduced both these species, and controlled hunting by humans, the wolves have been able to revert to preying largely on deer, along with wild boars. Since the reintroduction of deer, the wolf population has actually risen without causing problems for the shepherds.

Wolf numbers are now on the increase in several parts of Italy, and have risen from an all-time low of around 100 in the 1970s to an estimated 500 plus today. The increase has come as many rural districts have been abandoned by humans in favour of living in cities. The forests have since reclaimed land that was once grazed, and provided more space for wolves. The return of the wolf has caused tensions in areas where traditional shepherding practices have been lost. In some areas such as Tuscany, shepherds from Sardinia are often employed to tend the sheep, but since Sardinia has no wolves, the immigrant shepherds have no experience in training dogs to protect their sheep from wolves. They often suffer some losses as a consequence, especially if wild prey like deer are scarce. Their reaction to such losses is often to try and shoot the wolves, or to try and kill them with poisoned bait, a practice which affects not just wolves. The serious decline of many species, such as jackals and vultures, in the last century in some parts of Europe, including Greece, is linked to the use of poisoned baits.

The Abruzzo region is also rightly famous for harbouring the only significant population of bears, around a hundred or so, in Italy, along with some 600 Abruzzo chamois. The bears and wolves inhabit the great swathes of beech forest that cover the slopes of the steep and inaccessible mountains, and the chamois graze the high grasslands above the tree line. The region is strikingly beautiful, but this is no remote wilderness, since it has been populated by people for at least 5,000 years, and today the wolves are frequently heard howling in the valleys close to the roads and villages at night. One can also find plenty of evidence of bears, wild boar and deer visiting the same meadows by night that cattle and horses graze by day.

This close coexistence of wildlife and human culture has continued here, as in much of Europe, for millennia, and recently the relationship seems to be paying economic as well as aesthetic dividends. Despite much tension in the park's early days, when new rules on hunting and land use were first imposed, the local communities within the park have since prospered measurably. More and more visitors come each year to enjoy the park's beauty and wildlife, and thanks to them eating at the local restaurants and buying local produce, money has flowed into the region. One of the villages within the park, Civitella Alfedena, was recently identified as having the highest per capita bank deposit levels of anywhere in Italy! Several other villages that had once resisted becoming part of the park have since asked to be included. The region has succeeded in mixing conservation with prosperity, a combination which many economists and politicians claim is impossible; the example that the Abruzzo park has set may provide a model for the rest of the world to follow.

Evidence of another shy animal can be found in the Abruzzo's woodland, in the form of well-trodden trails through the woods, large mounds of soil and the occasional black and white, sharply pointed quill lying on the ground. Crested porcupines live here, although their main strongholds are in the gently rolling hills of Tuscany and low-lying coastal areas in the west and south of Italy. These animals are almost certainly of African origin, and most people believe that they were brought to Italy by the ancient Romans as food, but they either escaped or were allowed to establish wild populations (see box, p. 33: 'The Crested Porcupine').

The ancient Romans imported a number of animals and plants that they valued highly as food from around their empire, and many of these established populations that survive to this day. The list of imports includes the fallow deer from Asia, rabbits from Spain and carp from the Danube delta. Imported carp are common, alongside a host of other imported and local wildlife, in the marshes of Maremma. This is one of a series of low-lying coastal regions in Italy, now drained to a greater or lesser extent for agriculture, which were formed or added to greatly in ancient Roman times by huge quantities of silt washing down major rivers. The ancient Romans knew a lot about irrigation and terracing of fields, but they were unable to prevent much of the topsoil from agricultural land and deforested hillsides from being washed away during floods. The silt was sluiced down to the sea, and created a series of stinking,

mosquito-infested marshes on the coasts, the most extensive and notorious of which were the Pontine Marshes just south of Rome. Malaria became rife and ravaged the Romans, weakening them still further at a time when their empire was already in decline in the fifth century AD. They repeatedly tried and failed to drain the Pontine Marshes, but these, along with the Maremma Marshes, have only been drained effectively this century. Modern drainage schemes, and a small fish, *Gambusia*, which was introduced from South America to prey on the mosquito larvae, have seen off the malaria-carrying *Anopheles* mosquito only in the last fifty years.

Today, the surviving drainage channels at Maremma are alive with wildlife: edible frogs croak in the shallows, European pond terrapins bask on the shores, plopping into the water if alarmed, and dragonflies hawk over the water. Coypus, large aquatic rodents, chew at the reeds or swim past with babies on their backs or circling around them playfully. These animals are far more recent imports, and were introduced to Italy from South America in 1928 for their fur or 'nutria', but have since escaped and set up a thriving feral colony. The land surrounding the drainage ditches is a mix of umbrella pines managed for the pine nuts in their cones, and surviving marshland grazed by horses and dramatic long-horned Maremma cattle. Large numbers of wild boar live among the pine woods, and evidence of their diggings for roots and insects is everywhere. They come out into the marshy areas to graze alongside numerous fallow deer or to wallow languorously in muddy pools, especially in the cool and quiet of dawn and dusk.

Above left

Romulus, the legendary founder of Rome is depicted, suckling from a she-wolf alongside his brother Remus in many statues around the city.

Above right

The great vine terraces of Cinque Terre in north-west Italy reflect the order that the Ancient Romans brought to the land.

Above

A wolf emerges from the forest in Italy's Abruzzo Mountains to hunt for deer.

Above right

Wild boars tussle in the coastal marshlands of western Italy.

believed to have changed little some since Neolithic times, some 7–8,000 years ago.

The very continuity in the way of life here is the key to the *dehesa*'s huge diversity of wildlife. So regular is the pattern of trees, that it appears to be the product of an ancient tree-planting exercise on an enormous scale, but *dehesas* were actually created by the agriculturalists who first reached here and thinned out the original oak woodland. They are underlain by herb-rich pastures, cultivated cereals or Mediterranean scrub, and are managed carefully to yield a number of traditional crops. Cork, which provides a thick, fireproof layer around the trunk of the native cork oak, is stripped off every eight to ten years to produce stoppers for wine bottles, insulating material, shoes and even beehives. Thick branches are cut for firewood and to make charcoal, while thinner branches are made into *picón*, a fine form of charcoal used for cooking. This annual pruning also provides fresh leaves for animals to graze, and lets through more light to encourage pasture growth on which cattle, sheep and pigs can feed. Thanks to the extra light, many flowers grow here and insects thrive on the varied flora. Plentiful animal dung provides masses of food for lizards, snakes and dramatic birds like hoopoes, bee-eaters, shrikes and rollers, while cattle egrets and starlings follow cattle around to catch the insects they flush. Many birds such as hoopoes and little owls nest in crevices in *dehesa* oaks and ancient stone walls.

Birds of prey are also incredibly numerous. Red and black kites constantly cruise over the *dehesas* trying to spot nests they can raid within the crowns of oak trees, but are often repelled by noisy azure-winged magpies which share nesting duties in family groups. Short-toed eagles specialize in catching lizards and snakes, and feed them to their young. Large populations of griffon, black and Egyptian vultures benefit from carcasses of cattle and sheep they find in the *dehesas*, while the rare imperial eagle survives here by feeding largely on rabbits. Griffon vultures nest in large colonies on rocky crags, reaching their highest density in Extremadura within Monfragüe Park, which harbours about 400 pairs, along with over 200 pairs of black vultures – easily Europe's largest colony – nesting in large trees (see box, p. 37: 'European Vultures'). The view from the Moorish castle on the Monfragüe ridge is spectacular – *dehesa* landscape rolls away from you as far as you can see, and huge vultures with nearly 3m (9½ft) wingspans drift by at eye level less than 50m (160ft) away.

Enter almost any scrubby woodland in the rolling hills of south and west Italy, and you can find a network of trails running through the thick, brambly undergrowth leading to large burrow entrances, fronted by heaps of red soil. If grey hairs cling to brambles and fence wires nearby, the burrow is probably a badger sett. If flies buzz around the entrance, and it smells of rotting meat, the burrow belongs to a fox. But if the burrow smells clean and earthy, the chances are that crested porcupines live here. Scout around, and you may well find some sharp black and white quills lying on the ground. However, the chances of seeing a porcupine, even if you come back at night, are slim. Porcupines, despite their formidable spiny defences, are incredibly shy, strictly nocturnal animals. Their secretive habits make them one of Europe's least-understood mammals, even though they are becoming increasingly common in Italy, the only country where they are found outside Africa.

Thanks to recent painstaking studies in Italy, many details of the porcupine's remarkable lifestyle have now come to light. Porcupines appear to wake up around 6pm throughout the year, but always wait until dusk (which is several hours later in summer) before emerging. They search for fallen fruit, but are also great diggers. Their large, squashy noses are very sensitive to the presence of buried food, and they dig powerfully and rapidly to find roots and tubers. They will also raid farmland for maize, potatoes and other root crops. They live in small, close-knit family groups with their young. There are usually just one or two offspring, but occasionally there are up to four. The youngsters follow their parents around in single file, even once they are fully grown. Porcupines often argue noisily over a particularly prized piece of food, grunting loudly, stamping their hind feet and rattling hollow quills that make an unsettling sound rather like an angry rattlesnake. These warning sounds are no empty threats when a porcupine is in real danger. After a night out looking for food, the whole family always returns home before the light of dawn.

Porcupines can breed at any time of the year and often mate several times a night, both inside and outside their burrows. Mating seems to serve partly as a greeting ritual that reinforces very strong pair bonds and is not restricted to any kind of mating cycle.

Crested porcupines have been protected by law since 1974. Although they are still hunted for their meat in some regions, these curious African mammals are now well-established members of Italy's rich fauna.

NU

At night, the rare Iberian lynx sometimes prowls through *dehesas* for prey such as rabbits and hares. This animal is smaller than its northern relative, and has a richer, more strongly patterned coat and longer, beard-like tufts of fur around its face to complement its tufted ears. Nowhere common, its greatest strongholds are mountainous terrain and within the famous Coto Donana Park near Huelva in the south. The far smaller wildcat, and agile, rather cat-like genets are also active at night, taking mainly smaller prey such as mice.

The south-eastern part of Extremadura blends from wooded *dehesa* landscape into the drier steppe-like grasslands of La Serena, an extensive region of grazed pastures and wheat fields on rolling hillsides, which are exploited by a different array of creatures. Male great bustards perform their spectacular throat-ballooning, feather-ruffling displays here, and little bustards their comical leaps (see box, p. 84: 'Great Bustards'). Both birds will only display in wide-open areas where they can be seen by females, and where they can see ground predators approaching. This is also the stronghold of stone curlews, and of pin-tailed and black-bellied sandgrouse which regularly come to drink at watering holes dug for cattle.

Some *dehesas* have been reduced to grassland through overgrazing, but vast areas, including half of Extremadura's agricultural land, still survive in their ancient form, with new trees being allowed to grow up and replace old ones as they die off. The success of this original Neolithic system appears to have been accepted and adopted by the Romans, the Moors, and by medieval and modern farmers alike, until today when they are facing their greatest threat since the Ice Age in the form of recent Spanish and European agricultural policies. These favour and reward higher livestock densities than *dehesas* can withstand, and the vital regeneration of new trees is threatened. Further land has been turned over to intensively cultivated cereals, sunflowers and other irrigated crops, leading to a drop in surrounding water-tables on which much natural vegetation and traditional agriculture depend. There is growing international concern for this traditional landscape, and recent changes may yet be reversed to allow a tried and tested way of life which encourages such diverse and unusual wildlife, to be protected. Many of the old traditions are still adhered to, and some that were being lost are now being revived in their original form.

As summer warms up, hundreds of thousands of sheep and goats leave the plains of Extremadura for their annual journey to the lush mountain pastures of the Picos de Europa and the Pyrenees to the north. Although most sheep are now moved by road and rail, the old practice of driving the sheep for hundreds of miles along ancient driving routes or *canadas*, some of which cross bridges built by the ancient Romans, is being reintroduced in some areas. The sheep graze along the way, and by doing so, they keep the scrub down, and more flowering plants spring up the following year when a different route will be taken. The journey sometimes proves too much for the older and weaker members of the flock, and this is traditionally a time of rich pickings for the vultures. No carcass is left unnoticed for long, and within an hour or two of its discovery a sheep can be reduced to a bare skeleton by a frenzied horde of some thirty to thirty-five griffon, black and Egyptian vultures.

While the summer heat forces the great migrations of livestock to the mountains, a rather different migration, of tourists, moves in the opposite direction. People from all over the cooler northern regions of Europe flock to the warm beaches of the Mediterranean, often bringing them into close proximity with the wildlife riches of coastal lagoons throughout the region.

Perhaps Europe's most famous coastal wetland, where the juxtaposition of wildlife and tourism is obvious, is the Camargue in southern France where the Rhône forms an extensive delta, comprising a patchwork of natural lagoons and marshes alongside managed pastures and arable fields. While most of the tourists head straight for the beaches, some come to view the incredible diversity of bird life, which includes eighteen species of raptor, all nine European species of heron, egret and bittern and the region's most famous birds of all, the greater flamingos. The wide variety of land uses is the key to the Camargue's richness, with irrigation and drainage ditches, rice fields, permanently flooded marshes, seasonally flooded wetlands, brackish and saline lagoons all providing opportunities for different species. Recent increases in rice-growing and salt-drying have threatened the balance of habitats, but the salt companies have cooperated well with conservationists to protect breeding and feeding areas for the flamingos.

The Camargue is also famous for its native race of white horses, which roam semi-wild in the seasonally flooded rough pasture known as *sansoire*. Here, too, live many black Camargue bulls that are reared not for beef, but for the local form of bullfighting, in which the aim is not to kill the bulls but to snatch ribbons from their horns. The bulls are rounded up for the fights by local cowboys or guardians riding the white horses. The Camargue is an enchanting, if uncomfortable, place in the summer, when it is often stiflingly hot, and alive with mosquitoes and horseflies. Dragonflies dart in among the dancing flies to snatch their prey, while colonies of bee-eaters raise their chicks on both dragonflies and smaller prey. As summer turns to autumn, large groups of swallows start to gather in the Camargue, perching in the reeds and flying around in excited circles. It is a sign that the autumn migration of birds is about to begin, and all over Europe, birds both large and small begin to head south.

After Gibraltar, the greatest concentration of migrating birds anywhere in Europe occurs over the city of Istanbul, known in antiquity as Byzantium. Large soaring birds, such as storks and raptors, funnel out of Europe, passing over the narrow, 30km (18 miles) long stretch of the Bosphorus between the Black Sea and the Mediterranean, to cross into Asia on their way south to Africa via Israel or to southern Asia itself. By choosing a largely overland route, the birds can use thermals to get lift, spiralling up to a great height before gliding along without using much energy. On some days in September, the birds cross quite low over the Bosphorus, and groups of several thousand storks, up to around 150 Levant sparrowhawks, 50 honey buzzards and 30–50 lesser spotted eagles pass right over the Camlica hills on the Asian side of the river. Some 3–12,000 raptors of between 16 and 18 species may be seen here on the best days by observers, although a good telescope is often needed and city haze can spoil the views. On other days, easterly winds hold the birds back or, when the thermals are giving consistent lift, the birds pass over very high, and even eagles are mere specks in the sky. The overall impression, if you watch for a few days, is awesome, and the importance of the fly way is clear. It is reckoned that hundreds of thousands of storks and raptors pass this way between mid-August and mid-October.

Smaller birds are able to travel long distances by flapping their wings, rather than by soaring, and many take more direct routes to Africa by flying right across the open Mediterranean sea in a broad front. Many fall prey to the spectacular Eleonora's falcon, which breeds in colonies of up to 200 pairs on islands throughout the Mediterranean at this time of year and feeds its chicks on the migrants.

Far below the falcons' breeding ledges, loggerhead turtles swim effortlessly through the blue waters as they head for quiet beaches in the eastern Mediterranean on which to lay their eggs. Most of these marine reptiles spend the winter off the coast of Tunisia, but migrate across the Mediterranean to lay their eggs on beaches in Turkey, Cyprus, and several Greek islands, especially Zakynthos, between late May and August. The eggs develop over a period of two months, and from late July onwards, young turtles hatch at night and head for the sea (see box, pp. 125: 'The Loggerhead Turtle').

The young of an even rarer, and very odd-looking reptile, emerge on autumn evenings on a handful of beaches on Crete, the Dodecanese islands, and one mainland site in Greece. Tiny,

The Barbary Macaque

The Barbary macaque is Europe's only primate, and is better known to many as the 'Rock ape' of Gibraltar. However, although it resembles an ape – having almost no tail – it is in fact a monkey. There are some eighteen kinds of macaque worldwide, but while all the other seventeen species are found in South-East Asia, the Barbary macaque lives only in North Africa and on the Rock of Gibraltar.

The Barbary macaque is believed to have come from North Africa, and then to have expanded its range into Asia and Europe before the last Ice Age, which reached its peak around 20,000 years

ago. It is thought to be descended from ancestral macaques with long tails. Those macaques that came to inhabit cooler zones gradually lost their tails, perhaps to minimize heat loss and avoid frostbite. The species is native to Morocco and Algeria, but it is uncertain when it was introduced to the Rock of Gibraltar and by whom. Some believe that the macaques survived the Ice Age in southern Spain and Gibraltar, but they almost certainly retreated to Africa, and were only reintroduced less than 300 years ago by the British after they captured the territory.

The Barbary macaque is usually uniformly buff coloured, but individuals vary in colour from blonde to grey. As in most primates, males are larger and stronger than females. There are strong bonds between individual macaques, not only between males and potential partners and mothers and their infants, but also between females, among juveniles and between adolescent males. Most surprising, perhaps, is the relative lack of aggression between adult males. Unlike most macaques, the Barbary macaques live in troops including as many as ten adult males. Such troop composition is viable thanks to their unusual sexual system: an ovulating female will mate with more than one male, thus reducing the tensions between males. This may explain why male Barbary macaques are so famous for paternal care; several males could be the father of a particular infant.

During the Second World War Churchill's troops adopted the Barbary macaque as a symbol of British sovereignty and came to believe that the British would only surrender the Rock when the last macaque left. The macaques of Gibraltar seem unlikely to leave the Rock in the near future. Many of the 200-strong population are fed daily by the stream of tourists who visit them high on the upper rock. Most have become used to humans and many are proficient at prising food from unsuspecting visitors!

At one time, the Barbary macaque probably ranged over the whole Mediterranean region of North Africa, but today it only survives in a few isolated areas of scrub and remnant oak, cedar and fir forest. Estimates from the mid-1970s put the Moroccan population of macaques at 18,000 and that of Algeria at no more than 6,000. Furthermore, they are dispersed in just a few scattered relict habitats. Deforestation is still on the increase in Morocco and Algeria and the future of the species is by no means secure.

RP

European Vultures

The Cradle

You don't have to go to Africa to see large groups of majestic vultures circling overhead, or squabbling in noisy groups over a carcass. Four species of vulture nest in Europe: the black, the griffon, the Egyptian and the bearded, once known as the lammergeier, a name which is now discouraged since it erroneously alluded to them harassing lambs. Vultures depend strictly on carrion, and a recent claim that rogue griffon vultures were killing sheep for themselves proved to be a hoax. Far from being a threat to livestock, vultures are viewed in many regions as helpful because of the way they tidy up the carcasses of wild and domestic animals that have died.

The four species are all very different from one another. The black vulture is the largest and heaviest; in flight, its huge wings span nearly 3 metres. It has the most powerful beak and, where its range overlaps with other vultures, is often the first to tear open a carcass and expose the flesh below. They can displace other vultures from a carcass at will, including the griffon which, although nearly as big, has a far less powerful beak. Griffons specialize in reaching into an opened carcass with their long necks and pulling out the softer parts with their smaller, sharp-edged beaks.

The Egyptian vulture is a far smaller bird, easily identified by its largely white plumage and small pointed beak; it feeds on scraps and leftovers around a carcass, and specializes in scavenging generally. The rare bearded vulture is lighter in build than the griffon and the black. It has a long wedge-shaped tail and wings that are nearly as long as those of the black vulture. It moves in after the others have stripped a carcass bare, specializing in bones which it often carries to a great height to shatter on rocks below before swallowing broken fragments, even alarmingly large ones.

The success of vultures is linked closely to the way land is managed and to human attitudes towards them. They still live in huge numbers in areas such as Extremadura, the Picos de Europa and the Pyrenees. Here, large populations of domestic animals are tended in traditional ways, and vultures can find undisturbed nesting areas. A healthy population of griffon vultures survives on Crete, but there are far fewer now that pick-up trucks have replaced donkeys as the major means of transport. On mainland Greece, large vultures have become extremely rare, probably through feeding on poisoned bait put out to kill wolves and jackals. There has been a huge decline in vulture populations throughout Europe as 'pastoral hygiene' has been increased, and poisoned bait used.

Today, vultures are increasingly being provided with the protection they once lacked, and with food to maintain populations and to provide visitors with the chance to see them. Numbers are now creeping up in some countries; bearded vultures have been reintroduced in Austria and Switzerland and griffons have been reintroduced into the areas of France from which they had disappeared.

NU

swivel-eyed chameleons emerge in groups of 20–50 from the sand and head for the nearest vegetation, where they sit until dawn before heading off and blending into deep tamarisk scrub or reedbeds. They are fully formed and ready to catch flies a body-length away with their extensible, sticky-tipped tongues. Adults also come to the coasts around this time, to set up courting territories, where the males fight aggressively, lunging at one another and biting, while females look on and take their time before accepting a mate. The adults, which can be over 40cm (16in) long, are so well camouflaged that they are almost impossible to find even if you are looking in the right place. They can change colour within seconds to signal their moods or to blend in with changing backgrounds. How chameleons reached these scattered Greek locations, along with the southern tip of Spain, is still a mystery. They seem to be of African origin, and may have been brought as curiosities by the ancient Greeks, or perhaps the Romans.

Autumn in the Mediterranean is a very dry time; all the vibrant greens and splashes of colour from flowering plants that typified the spring have vanished, and the land takes on the yellows and golds of dried-out plants. But as autumn moves to winter, from late September onwards, the once blue skies of the Mediterranean fill with clouds and rain returns across the region.

The last of the migrant birds head south to their winter quarters, including one of Europe's most spectacular birds, the crane. This bird, which stands over 1m (3ft) tall, once bred in large numbers across much of Europe including Greece, Italy and Spain until the Middle Ages. However, a large number of its nesting areas were drained over the centuries to create more farmland, and so it became extinct in many countries. A greatly reduced population now breeds almost exclusively in north-east Europe. In the late autumn, their haunting, bugling calls are heard across much of Europe as they migrate in huge V-shaped groups. Birds from Sweden and Finland head due south, passing through central Europe and the eastern Mediterranean region on their way to their major winter quarters in the Middle East and Africa. But part of the Scandinavian population, some 60,000 birds, take a different route, heading south-west across Germany and France before arriving at their remaining Mediterranean winter stronghold in Spain, in Extremadura.

Most of the smaller, insect-eating birds leave for the warmth of Africa, but the cranes move in to replace them in the Spanish *dehesa* landscape that is now often shrouded in mist, and lashed by frequent rainstorms. Winter in the Mediterranean is more of a wet season than a cold one, and for many plants, this is the growing season, or the time when fruits ripen. For the cranes, the major lure is the acorn, the fruit of the innumerable oak trees that dot the *dehesa* landscape as far as the eye can see. The oaks flowered back in March and April and produced acorns that mature from the end of October to December. The acorns not only provide high-calorie food for livestock and wild animals during the harsh winter period, but are also a vital food source for the visiting cranes. The birds usually split up into family groups to feed beneath the oak trees, the adults carefully carrying acorns to depressions in the ground where they can hammer them open. They also pass them to their young, allowing them to learn how to crack these hard fruits into bite-sized chunks for themselves. Wintering robins sneak in to eat acorn fragments missed by the cranes. Nearby, large grey Iberian pigs snuffle through the pastures, gorging on the acorns which give *jamón Serrano* (Iberian ham) its distinct, rich flavour. Vast numbers of wood pigeons also come to the *dehesas*, gathering in vast roosts in the evening, where they are often chased by peregrine falcons who swoop down on them from a great height to make their kills.

In this cool, wet Mediterranean winter, only the mountain tops become frozen and snow-covered, and many flowers still bloom at this time of year. Winters in northern Europe, by contrast, are long, dark and bitterly cold. In April, just as the ice on the lakes is beginning to melt and the hours of daylight are increasing, thousands of people begin to gather on the shores of Lake Hornborga in Sweden. They await a great natural event that for them heralds the arrival of spring each year: the return of the cranes. Huge flights of cranes arrive on the shores of the lake to feed and to dance, and these boisterous courtship antics attract rounds of applause from the onlookers. These 'Swedish' cranes, arriving in the northern spring, are the very same cranes that confirm the arrival of winter in Extremadura, and which the Spanish view as 'theirs'. In truth, they are Europe's cranes, and their future survival depends on a unified approach to helping them. Encouragingly, countries along their flight path, such as France and Germany, are beginning to cooperate with Spain and Sweden in preserving safe places for the cranes to feed, roost and breed. These charismatic birds may perhaps inspire a number of coordinated projects to protect a wide range of species across Europe.

EUROPE'S LANDSCAPES AND WILDLIFE: ITS FUTURE

The landscape of the Mediterranean has undoubtedly been transformed over the last 8,000 years by the advance of agriculture, and the same process, adapted in various ways to different natural terrain, has swept through most of Europe since agriculture first reached the Mediterranean. The widely held perception that Europe's landscape has been largely ruined by the changes, and that an impoverished range of wildlife has been driven to the few remaining wild sanctuaries, hugely underestimates the enduring beauty and richness of Europe and its fauna. In the Mediterranean alone, many of the humanized landscapes are truly stunning, from the flower-carpeted olive groves of Greece, to the terraced hillsides of Italy and to the rolling vistas of oak-studded *dehesa* in Spain. Nor has all the spectacular wildlife been driven out of Europe, or into just the fragmented remnants of former habitats. Wolves and bears still inhabit managed lands, and many of Europe's plants and animals have found ways to take advantage of agricultural practices. The phenomenal diversity of Spanish *dehesa* alone shows that the changes can actually benefit many forms of wildlife.

The story of how landscapes changed, and how wildlife adapted, varies considerably in different kinds of natural habitat across Europe. The nature of the land itself – whether it was originally wooded, mountainous or flooded, for example – dictated how it could be modified by agriculturalists, and very different assemblages of plants and animals have been affected and have adapted more or less easily to change. The survival of so much wildlife across Europe is no reason to be complacent, however, for much of it is threatened. There is now an urgent need to discover as much as possible about the relationship between wildlife and habitat, both agricultural and more natural. Armed with such knowledge, we are in a better position to safeguard its diversity.

Cooperation between countries is becoming increasingly important in safeguarding the future of Europe's wildlife and its distinctive landscapes. A large number of birds and animals travel widely through Europe and many great mountain ranges, grasslands and woods also straddle various countries. A 'new map' of Europe, in which the landscape types, rather than political divisions, are paramount is now emerging. Protecting and preserving the key features of each form of land is the key to maintaining their vigour, along with that of wildlife, and ultimately of Europe's human population. We, too, depend on healthy landscapes and air for our survival. This is not to say that politics is unimportant, for in the same way that the attitudes of ancient cultures such as those of the Greeks and the Romans towards the natural world affected their use of land and their treatment of animals, so too are present-day views about nature and modern political policies crucial to the 'living Europe' that people inhabit today.

CHAPTER 2

LAST OF THE WILD WOODS

THE WILDWOOD

I t is woodland, perhaps more than any other habitat, that creates for us the most immediate feeling of contact with the original wilderness of an ancient and bygone Europe. Forests are places where wild things live; they can be seen as dark, dank and forbidding or as fresh, green and full of life. When the people of Europe were hunter–gatherers the forests were their home; trees then covered 80 to 90 per cent of the continent. Today, as we journey across this continent, we might glimpse a wooded landscape from a car or train window for no more than a kilometre or two before seeing the inevitable field, farm or village. In this heavily industrialized landscape we may suspect that there are very few truly wild or primeval woods left but, at least for a brief moment when we walk into any natural woodland, we do have a feeling of what might once have been the essence of the European landscape. To understand properly the nature of that primeval landscape we must search out and explore the remaining fragments of the mighty 'wildwood'.

As the warming climate released Europe from the clutches of the last Ice Age, 12–13,000 years ago, retreating glaciers exposed land that was quickly colonized by an advancing band of trees. Wherever temperatures rose to an average of 10°C (50°F) for at least one month of the year coniferous trees were able to

Above

Woodlands harbour all forms of life. Here, fungi spring from the base of a tree.

Opposite

Remnants of the ancient wildwood reveal the nature of primeval Europe.

Inset

The lynx – one animal which has come to depend on the last of the wild woods.

grow while in warmer regions the stronger-growing broad-leaved trees quickly dominated. Throughout the lowlands of the European peninsula there soon grew a blanket of mixed broad-leaved forests with oaks, elms and limes giving way to beech at higher altitudes while in the cold north, and on the higher mountain slopes, grew coniferous species such as Norway spruce and Scots pine. In the extreme south there were forests of evergreens like holm oak, Aleppo pine and maritime pine, which thrive in arid climates where beech and other broadleaves would soon wither.

That great wildwood has long since been swept away by an army of industrious people taking timber for building or for firewood, or clearing the land to cultivate pastures or crops. Today the forests that pepper our landscape are mostly forests that have re-established themselves, or have been planted on previously cleared land. Virtually all are managed to some degree for our own utilization and as such are a far cry from the primeval woodland that was once the essence of the European landscape. But a few relics of the ancient wildwood have survived and in these places we encounter the grandeur of the woodland habitat in all its glory. One of these forests stands out above all the rest. It is Białowieża Forest, straddling the border of Poland and Belarus in Eastern Europe. This 1,500sq km (579sq mile) forest is certainly the largest, and perhaps the only virgin old-growth wooded area in this forested zone of lowland Europe. It is by far the richest remaining fragment of the once extensive European wildwood. Here, like nowhere else, is revealed the nature and character of the ancient habitat that at one time cloaked an entire continent.

Białowieża's geographical location places it in a mixed forest zone: the deciduous trees of the central lowlands mingling with the conifers that become so abundant further north. The predominant species are hornbeam, oak, lime, pine and spruce. This living remnant of wildwood is a stronghold for animals that were once far more widespread when the continent was covered in trees.

A large tangle of twigs and branches balanced in the fork of a Białowieża oak is the untidy nest of a black stork. Four chicks silently wait for their parents' return. An adult bird circles above the trees to check for any danger before dropping down a short distance away and approaching the nest through the cover of the canopy. She swiftly regurgitates a meal of fish or frogs, then leaves to forage once more along the streams that flow through the wood. Black storks were once widespread through Europe but, unable to tolerate disturbance during nesting, they are now confined to remote forests in the east, plus an isolated population in Iberia.

Other creatures have been better able to adapt to new habitats, though the wildwood remains their ancestral home. The starling is a bird commonly associated with cities and it does so well there that it is easy to forget it is primarily a forest bird. There are several thousand pairs of starlings nesting in Białowieża, where they favour holes in old trees.

Not surprisingly, most of the wild animals and plants of the temperate part of the world are predominantly forest species. Even though the European forests have been ruthlessly cut, the wildlife heritage of Europe is essentially a forest fauna. So it is in the forests that we can begin to see the true relationships between so many of the creatures around us, and how and where an animal makes a living.

Many species are entirely dependent on the forest for their existence and they spend their whole lives there. Others may just rely on it for shelter, for nesting or for food. Either way, most of the creatures of the temperate world have evolved lifestyles of coexistence with trees. The forest is therefore of central significance in looking at the living creatures around us.

Białowieża Forest contains a reported 56 species of mammal; 226 species of bird have been recorded, of which 169 regularly breed. Over 8,500 insects have been identified although, as is the case everywhere with the smaller members of the animal kingdom, there are probably a good deal more that have gone undetected. Yet the forest is a secretive place: a first impression suggests there is very little visible life here. It is true that Białowieża is rarely silent, certainly in the spring when the calling and singing of birds seemingly emanates from every tree – but the songsters can be very difficult to spot. However, wait a while and the forest does slowly reveal a wealth and abundance of creatures. Listen carefully and you can tune in to new noises: the rustling of dry leaves discloses the presence of countless mice, voles and other small rodents. Come back at night and the birdsong has died away, but now there is even more activity on the forest floor. Mice, voles and dormice are most active under the cover of darkness.

Bank voles and yellow-necked mice are the two commonest rodent species in the forest and they can be present in impressive numbers. Bank voles are capable of reproducing once they are five weeks old, and with three to five offspring in a litter and up to five litters a year, populations can swell very rapidly. Their sheer numbers make these small rodents a very important element of the forest ecosystem, as they devour vegetation, buds and seeds. They are equally important as prey for many of the forest carnivores. Indeed, a year when rodents are particularly abundant is a bad year for many of the trees and plants, but spells success for a host of larger animals from weasels to eagles.

Weasels and stoats are specialist predators, their elongated bodies enabling them to squeeze through roots and branches on the forest floor in pursuit of their prey and even to follow them down their burrows. And many other carnivores, even wolves or goshawks, would happily take a mouse or vole if the opportunity arose, as it regularly does during a rodent year.

The numbers of rodents do vary from year to year, in a strangely regular way. Approximately every four years is a 'rodent year', when the populations of mice and voles explode. In other years there may be relatively few rodents; many perhaps are killed off by harsh winters or by a high predator population built up in a rodent year. It is a cycle of interdependence: a rodent year provides the predators with a lot of food and they themselves multiply faster; the next year this greater number of predators prevents the rodents from reaching such high numbers, leading in turn to a fall in the number of predators. Year by year the populations are changing and each population can affect the breeding success of many other species – not just the predators. Maybe one year there will be no new beech or oak seedlings because they will have been eaten by the rodents during their population boom. The whole forest can be affected by such population cycles of key elements like mice and voles.

Though a goshawk might grab a rodent as a snack, its more usual food is medium-sized birds such as grouse, pigeons and crows, which it can catch on the wing. It is well adapted as a predator of forest birds: its short, rounded wings and long tail enable it to twist and turn through foliage in pursuit of its prey, which it plucks out of the air with its powerful talons. In such a rich ecosystem it clearly pays to specialize in this way, while remaining open to other opportunities that may arise. Food *is* abundant, if you can find and catch it; be good at tracking it down and you won't go hungry. The lesser spotted eagle is a large predator that mostly feeds on small mammals, but during the breeding season it often specializes in taking frogs. At the time when the eagle has her growing chicks to feed, the frogs living in the forest all congregate together and announce their presence with a chorus of croaks. The lesser spotted eagle can often be seen standing in a marshy area, waiting to pounce on any amphibian that hops within reach. It takes other prey at times when frogs are not so easy to catch and has been observed standing outside vole holes waiting for the occupant to venture out.

Overleaf

In spring, the forest floor of Białowieża Forest.

The lynx was once a widespread European predator but persecution and the loss of its forest habitat have driven it to the remoter corners of the continent. There are scattered populations in some of Europe's wilder mountain ranges but, given that each lynx requires a territory of up to 1,000sq km (386sq miles), it is only these extensive northern forests that support a sizeable population. The taiga is the lynx's major European stronghold; it stalks these forests preying principally on hares, but also on rodents, ground birds (for example grouse) and sometimes roe deer.

The wolverine is another predator in these northern forests but, unlike the lynx, it has always been restricted to this habitat zone. It has large feet and a shambolic gait which enable it to gamble over the surface of the snow without falling through. It has a reputation for greediness; another name for the wolverine is 'glutton'. This was probably acquired thanks to its habit of killing more prey that it immediately needs and storing it under the snow. Great grey owls, Siberian tits and Siberian jays are all birds that are restricted to the taiga, living in these forests all year round. They have a thick layer of insulating feathers to keep them warm. But, of all the taiga specialists, one of the most secretive and most endearing is the small, furry, wide-eyed flying squirrel. This engaging creature sleeps through the winter in an old woodpecker hole and comes out at the first sign of spring to feed on the emerging buds and catkins. It is quite a little acrobat, scampering through the branches with incredible agility and, although not capable of true flight, it can glide between trees over 50m (164ft) apart thanks to a furry membrane that extends between the fore and hind limbs. The flying squirrel is, in Europe, restricted to southern Finland and the Baltic States of the former Soviet Union, but its numbers are declining as forestry practices remove old hollow trees where it rests and nests.

The ranges of Norway spruce and Scots pine, the dominant conifers of the taiga, have dramatically expanded through Europe in recent times (the twentieth century in particular). Together with a number of non-European exotics such as Lodgepole pine and Sitka spruce from North America, they are the chosen species for plantations: regulated forests of trees planted specifically for timber production. Thanks to the growth in the planting of these monocultures, woodland is currently the fastest growing habitat in Europe – recent trends indicate that there has been a 10 per cent increase of forest cover in Europe over the last thirty years. But these new forests have little in common with the virgin taiga. They are usually regimented rows of identically aged trees packed together and then cut down together. There is no natural death, decay or regeneration and very few other plants or animals can live here. These woodlands can be more sterile than a modern city.

Above

The flying squirrel relies on dead trees in which to nest. In managed forests dead wood is cleared, so these animals are rare in such areas.

Opposite

Though a highly efficient predator, the lynx requires huge territories in which to hunt its prey, especially during the winter months.

MANAGED WOODLANDS

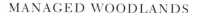

Though plantations can be found all over Europe, few people are fortunate enough to spend time in a primeval wildwood. For many Europeans, particularly those in the West, their

meantime there are opportunities for a whole succession of faster-growing plants to soak up the sunlight that is filtering down. 'Pioneer' species, such as birch, are fast-growing and they are able to flower and set seed before being overshadowed by the 'climax' species (the oak, hornbeam or other dominant trees). Many other plants adopt the same strategy: relying on growing up in openings in the forest and sending their seeds out to find new clearings before being ousted by slower-growing species. Thus the old forest is full of open glades, at varying stages of succession, which increase the richness of the flora and provide more grazing for the forest herbivores.

Storms can lay low large tracts of forest to create considerably more substantial gaps. Such gales would have created even more devastation in the past than the great storms of living memory, because in the truly primeval forest, unattended by man, trees of every age and condition, which would be fungus-ridden and rotting as they stand, would offer little resistance to very strong winds. This could cause a significant change in the forest itself.

What was a mix of hornbeam and oak could get blown away and a spruce forest might grow up in its place. Such a change could be brought about simply due to climatic variation. For example, a series of very cold winters during the years that new saplings are growing could favour spruce over the broadleaves. Within that forest the process of succession could lead to the emergence of many different species and compositions. This mosaic effect is enhanced by local variations in the soil type and water level. During the race to reach the canopy, different tree species may be favoured by different conditions. For example, certain species are particularly tolerant of waterlogged soil and consequently there are localized patches of alder, swamp or birch forest that are never succeeded by other species. This leads to the mosaic of habitats typical of a primeval forest. Thus, although a forest may be described as an oak woodland, this is only because in most places the oak is more numerous than anything else.

Below

The eagle owl, Europe's largest owl (which is capable of killing small deer), nests among tree roots on the forest floor.

The European Grey Wolf

Europe was once the domain of wolves. Their trails criss-crossed throughout the forests that covered its lands, from the lowland plains to the heights of the coldest mountains. The wolf's greatest success was its ability to exist in and exploit any habitat available. It is this adaptability that has ultimately saved the European grey wolf. In the Middle Ages wolves were persecuted. As forests were cleared, and with bounties set on their hides, their only escape was to the most inaccessible areas found in the mountains and the largest of the remnant forests.

Isolated populations of the grey wolf occur throughout Europe, but continuing persecution and habitat destruction means they are still under threat. It is only in the mountains of eastern and southern Europe that populations seem to be stable or on the increase. Their strongholds include the Carpathian Mountains, northern Spain and Poland. A European Wolf Network was set up by the Munich Wildlife Society in order to support conservation efforts and to monitor the status of the wolf in European countries by studying populations and their movements. From their stronghold areas wolves have begun to spread as young wolves try to colonize new territories. Wolves from Poland and the Carpathians have wandered into Germany, where they were once common, and also into the Czech Republic. Also, in a northward migration towards Germany's southern Alps, wolves have crossed over from Italian territories, moving up through the French Maritime Alps and Switzerland. Whether these new populations can become established in countries or areas still hostile to them has yet to be seen.

Studying the wolf in Europe can be extremely difficult, involving months of radio-tracking, and hiking through often hostile and remote areas to find carcasses left from their kills. Sightings of wolves are very rare. Field studies in Poland, however, give us a new insight into wolf hunting strategies. These wolves travel in smaller packs than those in North America, possibly because their main prey, the roe deer, is smaller. Nearly all of the kills occur in narrow valleys and, by following tracks in the snow, the researchers reconstructed dramatic hunts, discovering that wolf packs were using narrow valleys to herd their prey. Splitting into two groups, some of the wolves push the deer forwards down into the valley bottom while the rest run ahead on the hillside above. A wolf from the hill group suddenly leaps down, cutting off the escape route for the fleeing deer, which are brought to a sudden halt. The wolves at their rear charge into the panicked herd to secure their prey. If the deer escape and run on, then another wolf from the hill pack will descend until they either catch their prey or have exhausted their plan of attack, and themselves.

KJ

In early spring, before the forest giants have opened their leaves, the warming sunshine reaches into the woodland interior. Now is a time when the whole forest floor is bathed in light; a time of opportunity for those plants able to grow quickly enough to capitalize on it. A carpet of annual and herbaceous plants burst into flower, colourfully marking the end of the winter. But soon the trees' buds are opening and the new leaves begin to shade the forest floor once more.

This is when the forest birds establish and proclaim their territories. A dawn chorus in Białowieża reveals the impressive number and diversity of birds that nest here. Each bird is also busy checking out potential nesting sites, and in such a structurally complex habitat there are plenty of sites to choose from. Different species exploit different niches but they are all after the same thing: a safe and secure place to raise their young.

Hawfinches hide their nests in a clump of leaves or in a crook of a branch high up in the canopy. Lesser spotted eagles also nest in the canopy; although too large to conceal their whereabouts easily, there are few predators capable of reaching the nest *and* comfortably overpowering the formidably armed chicks, let alone the adults. Eagle owls are even larger birds but they don't make a nest at all. They will either commandeer an abandoned eagle or crow nest, or they will simply raise their young on the forest floor. The hazelhen is another ground nester; the precocious chicks leave the nest and follow their mother soon after they have hatched. The green sandpiper only ever nests in swampy regions of the forest while the pygmy owl nests almost exclusively in stands of spruce.

Woodpeckers, of course, create their own nesting sites by chiselling out holes in dead trees. Because each year they drill a new hole (sometimes they drill more than one before selecting a final site), they are a very important component of the ecosystem: their abandoned nest chambers provide many of the other forest birds, such as the collared flycatcher and the pygmy owl, with a place to rear their young. And because the ancient forest is full of dead wood, it is home to a lot of woodpeckers (which feed on invertebrates living in dead wood). There are eight species of woodpecker in Białowieża, and consequently it is just full of holes! (See box, p. 55: 'Woodpeckers'.)

Song thrushes also depend on dead trees for nesting sites. In Białowieża they nest almost exclusively in the walls of tangled roots of upturned forest trees. These exposed root systems are rare in managed forests and thrushes find alternative locations, but the primeval forest provides us with a picture of how animals originally evolved to make use of the different niches in the ancient architecture. They also provide us with a reference point from which we can measure the adaptation of creatures to the new landscapes we have created. Song thrushes now frequently nest in dense hedgerows, among creepers against a wall or on a vegetation-concealed ledge or bank – locations perhaps not so dissimilar from their ancestral favourite sites.

It has been suggested that the upending of trees, ripping their roots from the ground and taking a good deal of soil with them, is the primary way that the soil is 'tilled', because it is turned over and the organic material that accumulates on the surface is buried. Earthworms perform this function in the more open habitats that have replaced the wildwoods, rotating and aerating the soil as they burrow through it, but they are surprisingly scarce in the soil of an ancient forest.

The organic matter that litters the forest floor – the fallen trees, dead vegetation, autumn leaves and dead animals – is broken down by an army of tiny creatures: the detritovores. These range in size from the microscopic nematodes and rotifers to mites and springtails and the more familiar woodlice, millipedes, worms, snails and slugs. These in turn are food for a

Woodpeckers

Of all the hundreds of birds that can be found living in the woodlands of Europe perhaps those best adapted to this habitat are woodpeckers. Woodpeckers are specialists. They are perfectly adapted to a life in the trees: they have feet with two toes pointing forward and two toes pointing backwards for gripping on to trunks; a stiff tail to support them; short, rounded wings for manoeuvring through branches; a long, barbed tongue for extracting invertebrates from nooks and crannies; and, of course, a sharp chisel-like bill and reinforced skull for drumming on wood. If you watch a woodpecker probing for food by pecking away at dead wood to uncover grubs, it is easy to conjecture how this evolved into the excavation of nest holes and the territorial drumming that are the woodpecker's trademarks.

A drumming woodpecker is not actually drilling out a nest hole. The rapid-fire hammerings that echo through the forest in spring are males declaring their territories. Each male will have a number of drumming-posts chosen for their resonant qualities: these are branches that will transmit a deep and far-carrying sound. The nesting chamber is made by methodically chiselling away at soft dead wood. However, the exception is the black woodpecker which, being the largest and most powerful of the European woodpeckers, drills nest holes into living alder trees.

There are nine species of woodpecker in Europe, each with their own preference for tree species in which to nest. Five belong to the genus *Dendrocopus* – these are black and white birds with variable amounts of red on the head and under the tail. The three-toed woodpecker is a sixth black and white species, found in coniferous forests, and also birch and willows in the north. There are two European species in the *Picus* genus. These are green birds with red on the crown; they rarely excavate nest holes themselves.

Woodpeckers are more than just a group of birds perfectly adapted to their habitat; they are an intrinsic part of the forest ecosystem. The varied sizes of holes created by the different woodpecker species allow for a diversity of other creatures to make use of them, either for nesting or shelter. As the woodpeckers excavate new cavities each year their abandoned holes provide nest sites for birds such as flycatchers, rollers, nuthatches, wrynecks (a close relative of the woodpeckers) and flying squirrels. They also provide hibernation sites for bats, dormice and other small mammals.

Safe as a woodpecker's hole may seem, there are a number of predators to whom a small entrance-hole poses few problems. Martens and weasels, well adapted with their elongated bodies, have been known to prey on chicks and eggs hidden in woodpecker holes. However, one of the commonest predators of these chicks are woodpeckers themselves. Although their diet in the spring is largely made up of insects and other invertebrates it seems that woodpeckers will readily take nestlings of other birds nesting in their abandoned cavities.

JC

range of forest-floor predators: centipedes, beetles, spiders and even frogs and salamanders. But the true decomposers are the fungi (and the less visible bacteria), breaking organic matter down to inorganic minerals that can be absorbed by the network of plant roots which permeate the upper soil layers. The essential recycling process that they perform ensures the continual regeneration of the forest.

Białowieża has an enormous diversity of fungi of every shape and colour. Indeed, the richness of these decomposers is a measure of the primevalism of the forest. So easily overlooked, these important organisms really are a diverse group: from encrusting forms to bracket fungi and the classic toadstools. And these are just the fruiting bodies; the rest of the organism is a network of filaments threaded through the soil or dead matter, working year-round to recycle the woodland debris.

However, a few species of this rather unglamorous group are highly prized and specially sought out. A selection of edible mushrooms is harvested by people living in or by the forest. A particular favourite in Białowieża is the honey mushroom and, at their peak, favoured spots can become quite crowded with villagers collecting this tasty fruiting body. Even the bison find this species irresistible and every year they make a point of sniffing them out.

The honey mushrooms appear in early autumn and, apart from munching on these delicacies, the bison have other things on their minds: it is the time of the rut. This is when the usually solitary males join the matriarchal herds and form rutting territories. They churn up

Above

Bank voles are among the most common mammals in Białowieża Forest.

the soil with their horns and even uproot young spruce trees to demonstrate their strength. Occasionally two evenly matched bulls will fight for the right to court the females; this is an impressive sight. The whole forest seems to shake as two beasts of bone and muscle wrestle head to head, grappling with their horns as each attempts to push its opponent into a retreat. The winner will mate with the receptive cows in the herd. The calves are born in the following summer and remain with their mother for three years. The cows are very protective of their young and will charge if threatened. Today there are between 500 and 600 bison living in Białowieża Forest. But the population has not always been so healthy. The bison still roam Białowieża today thanks to the dedication of a team of scientists who kept the species alive (see box, p. 57: 'European Bison').

Two thousand years ago the bison was distributed throughout most of Europe, the only exception being northern Scandinavia. Hunting and, more importantly, clearing of its habitat ensured that by the end of the eighteenth century only two populations remained. These represented the two subspecies: the lowland bison in Białowieża Forest and the mountain bison in the Caucasus. The First World War spelt disaster for the lowland bison: a population of 700 animals crashed at the hands of the German soldiers and poachers, the last animal being shot in 1919. Poachers claimed the last wild Caucasian bison in 1926.

In 1923 a Polish scientist, Professor Jan Sztolcman, began a breeding programme involving animals preserved in zoos and parks. An initial census revealed a world population of 54 individuals; of these only 5 males and 7 females were of acceptable age and health to be included in the programme. In 1929 the first 2 animals, brought from zoos abroad, arrived in Białowieża Forest, the chosen location for the breeding, where they were housed in a specially built wooden enclosure. Ten years later the number was up to 16. In 1952, 2 animals were released back into the wild; these were joined by a further 38 over the following years. The first birth in the wild was recorded in 1957 and from then the recovery was rapid with a wild herd of more than 100 by 1965. Today, selective culling ensures that the population remains at a sustainable level.

Individuals from the Białowieża herd have been introduced into other forests in Poland and elsewhere in Europe, and the world population is now between 3,000 and 3,200 animals. These bison are all of the lowland race because, following their extinction in the wild, only one specimen of the Caucasian bison had survived in captivity. This bull was mated with female lowland bison and a population of around 200 of these hybrids now live in the northern Carpathians.

JC

Humans have had a further impact on the fauna, even in this hallowed wood. Aurochs, the ancestors of domestic cattle, were not saved from extinction and bears, wild cats, wolverines and European mink once lived here but were long ago hunted or harassed out of this forest. Conversely, the racoon dog and the American mink have invaded thanks to escapees from fur farms. And today, although the vegetation remains intact, the whole forest is dotted with grid-reference posts. Even in this, the greatest of Europe's primeval forests, one finds inescapable human influences.

Horses are not usually thought of as woodland animals, but the tarpan is a species of horse that was widespread in Europe at the time of the great wildwood. Unlike the bison it was not saved from extinction. Polish Ponies running wild in the forests south of Białowieża are the tarpan's descendants. The forest tarpan is actually a subspecies of the steppe tarpan, which wandered the wild grasslands around the Black Sea and eastwards. The last wild specimens were caught in Białowieża Forest in 1780 and transported to a zoo in southern Poland. When the zoo closed a few decades later the horses were given away to local peasants who valued their hardiness and crossed them with their domestic breeds. Attempts to re-create the forest tarpan through cross-breeding of the domestic animals that had wild tarpan blood began between the wars. Although complete restitution proved impossible, the resulting Polish Ponies have many of the tarpan's characteristics, including a short stocky build, long tail, their grey coloration and a dark stripe down their spine.

OTHER TYPES OF WILD WOODLAND

Today some of these ponies live in an ancient woodland: old-growth beech forests in the Roztocze Highlands, some 200km (120 miles) north of the Carpathian Mountains. Beech occupies a dominant position in European woodland ecology. Its tolerance to shade and the heavy shade it casts itself (which inhibits the growth of other species beneath its canopy), combined with its ability to grow successfully on a wide range of soils, has made it one of Europe's commonest broad-leaved tree species. The beech's sensitivity to summer drought and to flooding has enabled oaks and other associated species to flourish on the floodplains, but on higher and drier ground beech trees reign supreme. Their preference for hills and mountainsides has meant that they have fared better than lowland forest types: the terrain occupied by the beech has been a deterrent to many woodcutters due to its inaccessibility or the poor quality of the land once the trees are cleared. Consequently, several remnants of virgin beech wood have survived to this day.

Rich as these beech wildwoods are, they cannot compare with Białowieża. Their success at inhibiting the growth of other trees and plants beneath their canopy leads to something close to a beech monoculture with a relatively low diversity of plants. Furthermore, one of the key foods for many of the animals living in a beech forest is beechmast (the seeds of the beech tree), but this is produced very sporadically. In some years there is an abundance – far more than can be eaten – but in other years the forest produces virtually none. This irregularity in one of the major food supplies leads to a lower diversity of fauna in these woods. Having said this, a primeval beech wood is a magical place: smooth grey trunks stretching up into a dense canopy 40m (132ft) overhead; dead trees and fallen timber under attack from a host of insects and fungi; small rodents and larger animals such as wild boar and even bears searching for beechmast; while the chorus of birdsong in the spring can be a very lively affair.

There are even more extensive tracts of wildwood higher up on mountain slopes, although here it is the extremes of climate that make these forests rather less diverse than the likes of

Białowieża. As in the icy north, these mountain forests are dominated by conifers and, being relatively extensive and inaccessible, they often support good populations of large carnivores like lynx, bears and wolves (see box, p. 53: 'The European Grey Wolf').

The high mountain forests are in many ways reminiscent of the northern taiga, but there are some important differences. One of the most significant for the animals that live in these forests is the ease of escape when the harshness of winter sets in. Whereas the mountain fauna can simply move to a lower altitude during the winter freeze, animals of the taiga either have to migrate long distances, as many birds do, or sit it out. It is a tough time for the lynx which have to stalk snow hares and willow grouse in the cold, short winter days.

The trees themselves are well suited to the climate with branches and needles designed to shed snow, and resinous sap resistant to freezing. The broadleaves of Białowieża are not so well adapted to these conditions, although the winters here can be severe. They shed their leaves in autumn but their branches still catch the falling snowflakes. The weight of snow is a remarkable burden, especially for young trees only a few years old. With a thick layer of snow caught in their branches they may bow right down to the ground and, if they are held down throughout the winter, they will remain permanently bent until the snow melts. Consequently, the forest offers a record of its history of snowstorms in the form of trees with incredible arched trunks. These trees rarely survive for long but it happens regularly enough, so there is a continuing impression from the snow on the forest throughout the year.

This is the hardest time for the bison as well. Casualties could be considerable if it were not for the work of the forest guards who continue to put out food through the winter. This is no longer an exercise to ensure good numbers for the shooting season. These people are rightly proud of their mighty charges and of the greatest remaining relict of Europe's ancient wildwood that is now in their custody.

JC

Last of the
Wild Woods

CHAPTER 3

FRESH WATER

THE WETLANDS OF EUROPE

Perched on the peak of a thatched barn, with farmyard animals playing out their busy lives below, a brood of white storks look out from their nest at a watery landscape that stretches for miles to the flooded woods on the horizon. Waterlogged fields and reedbeds are marked only by the occasional line of fence-posts breaking the surface or by a hillock of high ground where rounded haystacks are safe from the damp. A double line of willows, snaking in parallel through the floods, reveals where the true course of a river lies.

These are the Biebrza Marshes in north-east Poland. They are suggestive of an early lowland landscape because, unlike virtually every other flood plain in Europe, the ways of these waters have been little altered by humans. The people who call this waterscape their home have adapted their lives to follow the rhythms of the river.

Where there is water, there is life, and this untamed wetland supports a diversity of plants and animals that far exceeds that of the dry land around it. At the height of summer, the croaking of frogs, screeching of terns, trilling of warblers, booming of bitterns and the drone and whine of innumerable insects merge into a heady chorus that dances across the water and rises to the storks and eagles circling overhead. These are all creatures that depend on an aquatic habitat for feeding or breeding and, along with numerous other plants and

Above
The Biebrza Marshes.

Opposite
The Biebrza Marshes are one of Europe's last untamed river valleys.

Inset
An otter, one of Europe's most elusive animals.

animals like them, are a testament to the richness of the wet habitats that once saturated this diverse continent.

The flooding of the River Biebrza is an annual event. Every spring, meltwater that runs off the wintry peaks at its source causes the river to break its banks and spill over the surrounding land, breathing new life into these wild marshes. This is the natural cycle of events that sustains an inland 'wetland', which is a lowland area periodically inundated by water. But this is just one of the many habitats created by freshwater.

Fresh water not only sustains a richness of life, but also scours, cuts, moulds and shapes the very landscape itself. Melted snow and rain flowing along rivers from the mountains to the coast, pausing in lakes, seeping underground, flooding the lowlands and dispersing into coastal deltas, creates a diversity of habitats where a multitude of life-forms flourish.

WATER AND LIMESTONE

The power of water can be seen in every gorge and valley that cuts its way into the heart of a mountain massif. The upland landscape has been sculpted by the increasing cycles of rain, snow and ice falling on to rock and flowing down to the lowlands. Rivers twist and turn through rocky terrain, picking up sand and silt and washing along stones and boulders as they journey down to the plains. The waters, with their mineral load, wear away at the rock they flow over, widening and deepening the channels that contain them. Glaciers, slow-moving rivers of solid ice (far commoner during the Ice Ages) are even more effective at reshaping their surroundings. They grind rock against rock as they transform narrow passages into wide U-shaped valleys. Some landscapes are especially susceptible to the weathering effects of water – limestone regions in particular. Limestone, or 'calcium carbonate', is a rock with a special property: it is soluble and it is therefore rapidly eroded by streams and rivers.

Where a river flows from hard rock to softer rock such as limestone, the softer rock is washed away more quickly, causing a sudden drop in the riverbed and resulting in a waterfall. Here the pounding water reveals its true force. It is a real contrast to the tranquillity of bubbling streams and lowland ponds and rivers.

In the northern Dinaric Alps of Croatia are some waterfalls of a rather special nature. The falls that link the Plitvice Lakes, strung along the River Korana are created not by a change in the underlying rock but by the depositing of stone walls over which the waters must flow.

This is a 'karst' landscape, a region dominated by limestone, and as the Korana flows through the soluble rock its waters become saturated with dissolved calcium carbonate. Where the waters flow over mosses and other vegetation, such as on the overgrown lips of the waterfalls, the limestone comes out of its solution and is deposited on the surface of the plants. This is caused by the aeration of the water and by the biological process of the plants breathing. The vegetation takes carbon dioxide from the water, so lowering the amount of dissolved limestone that the water can hold. As the layers of calcium carbonate build up on the surface of the plants, they consolidate into a wall of stone, or 'travertine' and fossilize the underlying vegetation in incredible detail. These stone walls are continually growing – at a rate of up to 3cm (1¼in) a year. As each barrier grows the water finds alternative routes down, initiating the creation of new falls. These are therefore truly 'living' waterfalls; rather than yielding to the rushing water, the limestone is growing and building itself up to form new barriers that divert the river this way and that.

Other limestone structures are far more common, although perhaps they are almost as rarely encountered, for they are made underground. Aside from its solubility, limestone has another special property: it is porous. Instead of washing over the land's surface, rain falling on limestone tends to seep down into the rock. Here it hollows out tunnels and caverns through which underground rivers flow and in which still lakes sit in the darkness. The incessant drip of calcium-saturated water forms stalactites that hang from the underground ceilings and, where the drops fall on rock, stalagmites grow up from the floor. As these continue to grow they will eventually join to form a stone pillar that reaches from the floor to the ceiling. There are waterfalls here as well, and they also grow as the limestone builds up on their lips. But they tend to be on a smaller scale; hundreds of miniature pools, held by tiny dams, cascade down a rock-face.

At their best, these formations are truly awesome. Giant caverns filled with crazy sculptures combine undeniable beauty with a rather sinister feel. Early cavers of the seventeenth century, when exploring the mighty Postojna caves in Slovenia, feared they had stumbled upon the entrance to hell. This dark place is not an eternal inferno, but on encountering the inhabitants (there is life even here, and a diversity of it) it is easy to believe that you have entered the house of the living dead. For this forest of demented pillars and spires is a fitting home for some of the most bizarre creatures to be found in Europe.

There are beetles and centipedes, aquatic isopods and other crustaceans that look in many ways similar to their above-ground counterparts, but they are drained of all colour. Other creatures bear little resemblance to anything up on the surface. Caves have long been known in folklore as the favoured haunt of dragons and so it is no surprise when the young of these legendary beasts were said to have been discovered in subterranean Slovenia. Ghostly pale, with two dark spots beneath their skin where eyes should be, stunted legs and pink protuberances on the sides of their heads, these elongated animals snake through the pools and streams in the cave systems of the northern Dinaric 'karst'. Since their initial discovery these 30cm (12in) long 'baby' dragons have been re-identified as a strange species of cave-dwelling amphibian and renamed the 'olm'. The olm's pink, feathery head-gear are external gills, similar to those found on the immature forms of better-known amphibians; the olm never leaves the water and retains its gills throughout its life. Its short legs aid it when clambering between underwater rocks but it can also swim, eel-like, through open water.

Despite their appearance all these cave specialists are healthy creatures. In the darkness deep underground there is no use for colour, so they waste no energy producing pigments. Eyes are equally useless; most of these creatures are therefore blind, their eyes being either degenerate or totally absent. Instead, many have long, sensitive feelers for finding their way and their food.

Very little is known about the lifestyle of such creatures. They may be blind but they are still able to sense light – and they do not like it. This makes the observation of their natural behaviour extremely difficult. Add to that, these animals are reluctant to do anything in a hurry at the best of times. Time runs at a different speed down in the depths of the underground world: it passes extremely slowly. The entire community depends upon detritus washed down from the world above, and its delivery can be an irregular event. The life here could never be described as abundant and predators like the olm may have to wait a very long time before a meal comes their way. This is exacerbated by the constantly changing water levels, which may cut the olm off in an isolated pool for weeks or months at a time, where the food reserves are quickly depleted. Theirs is a life of brief activity, interspersed with long periods of waiting. An olm is capable of going for several years without food and can live for a hundred years or more.

Recently a new race of olm was discovered, one with eyes and a heavily pigmented skin. It was found living in pools *outside* the entrance to a cave not far from the Postojna caverns. This seems to be evolution gone in full circle: a cave amphibian that has turned its back on its dark past and re-evolved to live a life in the sun.

LAKES

Rainwater, on its downhill journey to the sea, may seep into the earth and travel underground or it may run in overland rivers. But in places the land arrests its journey, storing up water in pools, ponds and sometimes the vast lakes that nestle in the folds of a mountain landscape.

The golden light of dawn dances over the ruffled surface of a giant lake – water stretching to the horizon like an inland sea. Silhouetted reeds are rocked by the waves, which paint ever-changing patterns on the white stones below. This is the ancient Lake Ohrid; set in the mountains of the Balkan peninsula, on the border between Macedonia and Albania, it is the third-oldest lake in the world, after Lake Baikal in Russia and Lake Tanganyika in East Africa.

With only a few streams feeding and draining it, this mighty lake, together with the creatures that make it their home, have been cut off from the rest of the world for millennia. Though not present in abundance, many of the animals that survive in these expansive, cold and nutrient-poor waters now live an existence not shared by any other organism on earth – they are unique. Ohrid is their universe. Here, generation upon generation of their ancestors have lived and died in isolation, cut off from any outside influences. Each species has followed its own evolutionary line, diverging away from the likeness of its relatives in the wider world. Though there are some more cosmopolitan species present in the Ohrid as well (recent colonizers or species that have changed little either in the lake or outside it), more than 90 per cent of the invertebrates and 60 per cent of the fish that live here are found nowhere else.

Strange flatworms glide over Ohrid's stones, wearing their own uniform of spots and squiggles, grazing on their own special menu of algae and micro-organisms. Endemic worms and molluscs siphon in the clear waters, straining out edible particles while they themselves are food for fish such are the Ohrid barbel, Ohrid bleak and the Ohrid salmon.

Unlike its better-known relatives, the Ohrid salmon does not migrate but spends its whole life within the confines of these Balkan shores. Just like its cousins it is considered very good eating and it has been dinner for people over the ages who have made these shores their home. Archaeological evidence shows that Neolithic man once fished these waters and his descendants have been doing the same ever since. Today the salmon fishery is an important source of employment and income for the towns and villages that have grown up around the edge of the lake. The fishermen still row out in their wooden boats to set their nets as their ancestors have done for millennia.

In January the fish are easy to find and on a calm day they can be spotted from the lake shore. Pairs of salmon are clearly visible in the crystal-clear water but no fishing is allowed at this time, for the fish have come to the shallows to spawn. The female salmon meticulously cleans a circular arena on the lake floor: every speck of algae is nibbled from the rocks to leave a gleaming white circle. All the while the male jealously guards the female and her territory from the attentions of other males. When the area is cleaned to her satisfaction, the female releases several thousand sticky eggs. The male fertilizes the eggs, and both fish cover them with sand and gravel.

Overhead, flotillas of water birds are riding the waves. There are tufted ducks, pochard, mallard and shoveler in mixed crowds; the number of coots alone runs into thousands. Having retreated here from icy waters further north, they sit out the winter on this lake, which is large enough and deep enough – and sufficiently far south – never to ice over, despite its altitude of 695m (2,293ft).

On the Greek–Macedonian border, 160km (96 miles) to the east, lies another large lake that provides a stark contrast to Ohrid. Lake Dojran is a lowland lake sitting in a shallow depression to the south of the Rhodope Mountains. Fed by nutrient-rich rivers flowing from the surrounding hills, these waters are warm, shallow – the maximum depth is 10m (33ft) – and hold an abundance of aquatic life.

A series of low islands along the edges of Dojran provide resting places for a group of noble-looking birds. These are Dalmatian pelicans, the rarer of the two pelican species that are found in Europe. These birds are threatened globally because of drainage to wetlands where they breed, but small numbers (around a hundred, which is 5 per cent of the European population) spend their winters here. Large numbers of cormorants, herons, egrets and gulls stand nearby, but they retreat as another flotilla of pelicans arrives at the shore.

Fresh Water

Below
The olm lives a life of eternal darkness in the depths of Slovenian caves.

Above
Over 3,000 pairs of white pelicans still nest in the Danube delta.

The white sands beneath the birds' feet hint at the enormous productivity of these waters. The little islands and every beach along the shoreline are entirely composed of broken and bleached shells, washed up from the central regions of the lake where countless thousands of freshwater bivalves carpet the shallow bottom.

The birds themselves are attracted here by the abundance of fish; Dojran has one of the highest densities of fish of any naturally stocked body of water in Europe. It is no surprise that a commercial fishery thrives on these shores. The techniques used by the fisherman have changed little over the years, for they work well and are in perfect harmony with the character of the lake and its inhabitants.

Extensive reedbeds fringe the shallow lake edges and the fish find shelter here from the flocks of birds that cruise the surface and stalk the shore, the dense reeds make fishing with nets or line impossible so the ingenious fishermen have come up with alternative methods. They partition off a section of the reedbeds, known as a *mandra*, with a series of *lesa*. These are fences made from tightly woven reeds. Cormorants, grebes, ducks, and whatever other water birds they have succeeded in catching with specially constructed traps placed where the birds roost, are then released into one of the partitions, or *parcela*. As the birds begin to dive for food, the fish escape through a small gap in the fence into the next *parcela*. The gap is closed and the birds are set to work in the next partition. In this way all the fish in the *mandra* are driven into a single *parcela* from which they can be scooped out with ease using hand nets.

In years of drought, when the water levels remain low and the reedbeds never flood, the fishermen employ different techniques. They provide the fish with a place to hide in the open water in the shape of a pile of twiggy branches called a *naseka*. The natural fishing activities of birds help to concentrate the fish here. The fishermen then surround this fortress with *lesa*, haul out the branches and scoop up the fish with hand nets.

The fishermen also use more ubiquitous methods, setting nets in the open lake. But here their previous allies, the birds, become their competitors and the lake is forever ringing with the cries and clanging of fishermen trying to keep feathered fishers at bay.

FLOOD PLAINS

Not all bodies of water are as permanent as Dojran and Ohrid. Approximately 1,400km (840 miles) to the north, water flowing from the hills and plains of north-east Poland once again transform the Biebrza Marshes into a vast 'lake' – but a temporary one.

A furry nose pushes its way out from the dense reeds. Button eyes scan over the expanse of rippling water. Stumpy legs launch the bulky body from the shore and webbed feet power the beaver out across the extensive marsh, steering with her broad tail. She stops where the roots of a willow trawl the surface of a flooded channel, and clambers out on to the bank. Her long yellow teeth chew the leaves from the twigs of the willow sapling. Disturbed by a noise, she drops back into the water and is gone; only the mangled skeleton of the young tree is evidence of her passing.

The noise is made by a horse and cart splashing along a submerged track in the marsh. The farmer is going to collect hay from a stack on a hillock that rises proud of the floods. It is for his cattle, which are still in their winter barns. Although the days are getting longer and warmer, there is no grazing for them: their pastures are all submerged.

It is early spring in the Biebrza Marshes and the floods are at their peak. Swans, ducks and geese float on the waters that have swallowed up the fields and wilderness of this untamed flood plain. It is this seasonal event that dictates the pace of life in the marshes. The growth and flowering of plants and the breeding, feeding and migration of animals are all constrained by the rhythm of the river. As spring advances and the waters begin to recede, all the life of the marsh is gearing up for the explosion of summer.

The frogs are already under way. Half of the European species of frogs and toads live in this wetland, and they all require shallow pools in which to breed and lay their spawn. The floods provide them with numerous opportunities, and the evening chorus of male frogs and toads staking their claim for the right to mate with every passing female is a clear sign that spring has arrived. Their frenzied activity will continue well into the summer although, as the waters retreat, they will be concentrated into smaller pools (see box, p.69: 'Frogs and Toads in Europe').

As the water-level drops, grasses and other low vegetation begin to appear. These small islands of turf in the waterlogged fields become theatrical stages where male ruffs claim a space on which to display their extravagant plumes to any reeve (female ruff) that might be watching, in what is known as the 'lek'. The males' neck ruffs, which give the birds their name, come in a range of shades and patterns and, together with their equally variable bulbous 'ear-tufts', there are rarely two birds looking the same. The lekking males fluff up these fancy feathers to intimidate their rivals and thus secure their patch of ground, and to impress the reeves that walk among the pouting males, assessing which male would be the most suitable father for their offspring. Having made her selection, a female crouches by him, accepting him as a mate. However, she will get no help from him in raising the brood because as soon as they have mated he continues to strut ostentatiously in front of all the other females still prospecting for mates. What she will get is sons with some of the characteristics that made her mate successful.

Most of these ruffs and reeves are only here in passing, as they are on their way to the tundra of Scandinavia and Russia. They are establishing a dominance hierarchy, and even mating, in preparation for their arrival at their northerly breeding-grounds where the short summer means that timing is of the essence. But there are other birds lekking in Biebrza and which do stay to nest. Female great snipe watch as groups of males perform an extraordinary display in which the vocals are every bit as important as the actions. The males, with puffed-out chests, sing an extraordinary song reminiscent of a rapidly bouncing ping-pong ball, or a one-note xylophone. Elsewhere there are arenas where groups of blackcock fan out their tail feathers, droop their wings, and emit a sound something akin to the bubbling of boiling water, interspersed with an excited 'tu-shhh', which is accompanied by a flicking of the wings and maybe a jump into the air. Running with short steps, they appear to glide back and forth over the short turf, looking just as if they are on miniature roller-skates. As in any lek, threat displays can occasionally turn into real aggression: two males may strike out with beaks, wings and feet until one of them backs down and retreats from the scene. The hens watch these contests with interest to see which male is victorious. If she is pleased with the winner a hen may invite a mating by crouching before him while he circles in front of her to pronounce his success.

Having mated, the female great snipe selects a site for her nest – the receding waters have now exposed larger areas of suitable ground. The marsh is dotted with the nests of other snipe, godwits, lapwings, redshanks and the wading birds that favour this wetland for rearing their chicks. These birds are proving that there is safety in numbers. Nesting alone they would be very vulnerable; in the short grasses of the marsh they would be a target for any predator that passed by. But, as a group with many pairs of eyes, they are quick to spot danger and are able to react to it.

A marsh harrier quarters over the ground for short-tailed voles (by far the commonest rodent in the marsh), other small mammals or bird chicks as it approaches the colony of waders. A godwit is the first to sound the alarm; it flies up off its nest, calling loudly. Soon the

air is full of wheeling birds screeching a warning and mobbing the harrier until it has retreated out of harm's way.

Marsh terns (both black and white-winged black terns) also nest in colonies for precisely this reason. They have no tolerance of anything that might be considered a threat, and they are fearless in their attack of intruders. They will fly at a farmer as readily as at a harrier, and even at his cows, which pose the very real threat of crushing eggs or chicks under their hooves. Few animals linger in the midst of a tern colony for long.

Another predator of the marsh is the short-eared owl. Unlike most owls this silent hunter patrols the flood plain during daylight hours, although it tends to be most active as dusk approaches. It glides over grazing land and reedbeds listening for short-tailed voles and other small rodents, which it will pounce on with deadly accuracy. The female carries her catch back to her chicks whose nest is well hidden in long grass in a scrubby corner of the wetland. Safe nesting sites are not too easy to come by in this flat, wet landscape (see also box, p. 72: 'The Eurasian Bittern'). The short-eared owl is careful not to give away the location of her chosen position, and once on the nest, she remains very alert for several minutes before settling down to brood.

Rather more conspicuous is the large, untidy nest of the white storks. Balanced on their chosen rooftop, the chicks are safely out of reach of most prowling predators. The protective adult birds with their dagger-like bills are also more than a match for any winged adversaries. The young storks are already well developed and have formidable beaks themselves; out in the marshes both their parents are collecting their next meal.

Below the nest, a farmer is preparing to take his cows to fresh pasture. He leads them out of the barn, which has confined them all through the winter, and down to the river where they

Frogs and Toads in Europe

A swollen river meanders slowly through the flooded forests of Austria, around swamped tree-trunks, through low, water-swept branches and under the higher boughs where storks and herons nest. All around, the air reverberates with a high, echoing hum. It is the song of the toad.

The fire-bellied toad, found across the wetlands of Europe, is one of the more aquatic of toad species. They only emerge on to land if they are forced to when the waters dry out – then they must find a muddy refuge. Their calls can be heard throughout the day and into the evening, providing a vibrant undertone to the screeching herons and the flute-like call of the orioles flying overhead. However, it is only the male toads that are noisy. Resting on floating plants or among the flooded marsh flowers near the banks, they bob up and down as their air sacs fill and empty like bellows. By calling out they are staking their claim to a territory and hoping to attract the females into it. The females spawn several times a year in a territory from April and through the summer.

The male toad's burp-like love songs are made by pumping air to and fro between the lungs and the vocal sac. The pitch of a male's croak is important because it changes with body size. Larger males have lower-pitched croaks and a male can judge the size of an opponent by its pitch when disputing over territories. There are rarely fights; the smaller males usually back off, although some have adapted to using a different tactic. 'Sneaky' males will wait silently in the vicinity and, as females approach, will try to jump to the head of the queue by mating with them before the territory owner has a chance.

Europe is essentially a very wet continent and once had huge areas of habitat suitable for its amphibians and other wetland wildlife. However, across the ages the people of Europe have dramatically altered their environment. Wetlands have been drained, filled in, reclaimed and ploughed up to enlarge or improve agricultural lands. Relatively recently, both agricultural and countryside management have changed enormously, increasing the devastation of many wetlands. Ponds and ditches once used for watering livestock are now replaced with troughs, and with the increased use of chemicals in farming those ponds that are left have become highly polluted. Contaminated waters drain into them and chemicals such as pesticides and fertilizers become concentrated. Fertilizers cause algal blooms. When the masses of algae die and decompose the processes take up all the oxygen in the water and so the animals living in the pond begin to die and the water turns stagnant. The Norfolk Broads in England, an important wetland site, have been severely damaged by this.

Surveys show that in rural areas frog and toad populations have plummeted and except for small, isolated colonies there are very few left. In huge areas throughout lowland and wetland Europe amphibians and other freshwater wildlife have either disappeared or become very rare as the habitats have diminished.

In towns, however, it is a different story. These animals have begun to prosper in artificial garden ponds. Gardens are now extremely important habitats for European amphibians. If it were not for gardens, parks and allotments that either have ponds or are situated near to them, some people believe that many amphibians would now be extinct across large areas.

KJ

Above
A marsh frog.

Opposite top
The European beaver is an extremely territorial animal; it will scent-mark trees and stones to make claim to a territory.

Opposite bottom
Though surrounded by water, the hay is dry, and is held above the flooded Biebrza marshland on little hillocks.

are herded on to a barge. The cattle are then punted across the flowing river to newly exposed grazing land beyond. The pastures are very rich thanks to the nutrients that the floods deposit each year, and the farmer is able to produce plenty of hay with which to feed his animals when their fields are under water. But most of the Biebrza flood plain is too wet for the farmer to grow crops, and late floods restrict the grazing season for his livestock. It is in breaking free from subordination to the vagaries of the annual floods that people have caused the ruin of so many of Europe's marshes. By building river defences and digging drainage channels throughout a marsh they ensure dry land all year round. The price they pay is the loss of the natural fertilization of the fields by the floods, so manure or chemical fertilizers have to be applied to keep the fields productive. The floods that fill the Biebrza Marshes remain untamed to this day.

With the advance of summer, the waters have receded and the river is contained within its banks once more. The vast lake of early spring has transformed into a patchwork of wet habitats. Pastures and hay meadows nestle against reedbeds, swamp forests and extensive areas of waterlogged sedge and grass. Among these there is a network of permanent waterways and pools – home for the truly aquatic creatures of the marsh.

A fisherman casts a line from his boat on a backwater of the Biebrza. Eyes fixed firmly on his float for the sign of a bite, he is unaware of the hidden struggles of life played out beneath the surface. A shoal of fry twitches nervously as the young fish pluck tiny creatures from the waters that flow past them. Dangers lurk in the thick vegetation that lines the underwater bank: sharp-toothed perch and pike wait to ambush any unwary fish that drifts past their jaws. Down in the darkness of the riverbed a group of bream stir up the muddy bottom as, with tails pointing to the sky, they mouth through the silt in a search for food. Up above them cruise shoals of bleak, their upward slanting mouths adapted for sucking down flies that land on the surface.

The water surface itself provides a unique environment inhabited by a few specialist invertebrates. Pond skaters walk on the water with the aid of dense pads of hair on the underside of their legs. They feed by sucking the juices of dead or dying insects that have fallen on to the surface. The much larger raft spider is more predatory. It breaks through the surface tension to grab small fish or invertebrates that swim up beneath it. There is another spider, the water spider, that actually lives under water, trapping air in its abdominal hairs and storing it in a silken bell attached to an aquatic plant. It too preys on small fish and other aquatic life. The water spider is just one of a number of ancestrally terrestrial creatures that have discovered new opportunities beneath the surface. But some of the animals that share the spider's brave new world have ambitions to leave.

The segmented bodies of mosquito larvae hang tail up from the water surface. By wafting the short bristles around their heads they induce small currents from which they sift minute food particles, while breathing through a tube that pierces the water's surface. Like many other marshland insects, these aquatic larval forms pupate into winged adults that, in the summer, leave their watery world for a life in the skies. At the peak of their emergence mosquitoes cloud the sky as they swarm over the wet landscape in their thousands. All red-blooded creatures suffer from the attention of the females, hungry for blood to fuel the production of their eggs. Interestingly, the males live entirely on plant nectar.

Clouds of a different kind instil a pause into the hustle and bustle of summer. A myriad of insects and many other animals take shelter from the heavy rain but, perched up on its rooftop, the white stork's nest is fully open to the elements. The nest-bound fledglings look thoroughly miserable and increasingly bedraggled as they are pelted by the storm.

For the storks this is just a passing discomfort, but for other fledglings the rain could pose a real danger. The terns and waders are nesting on land exposed by the retreat of the spring floods. Now, rainstorms throughout the River Biebrza's catchment area could cause the waters to rise again. Daily fluctuations in the water-level are caused by the variable weather conditions in the region, but a prolonged spell of wet weather could result in the flooding of nests and burrows and the consequent drowning of chicks, young rodents and other animals breeding underground. The farmer on whose barn the storks are sitting out the storm also has cause for concern. Dependent on the silt deposited by the spring floods to fertilize his land, he is equally at the mercy of the changing water-levels throughout the summer, for he needs access to his grazing lands and his fields must dry out if he is to make hay later in the year. Luckily for the farmers, and for the wildlife of the marsh, summer floods are rare.

The heat of the midsummer sun continues to dry out the wetland. Pools that have been a nursery for hundreds of tadpoles and several generations of mosquitoes rapidly shrink. Late tadpoles face a race against time: they must grow and metamorphose into froglets capable of surviving on land before their home evaporates from around them. Baking in the drying mud is one fate, but they are more likely to provide a foraging bird with a meal because, as their pool disappears, they are left with nowhere to hide.

Across much of the marsh, however, the ground remains sodden. Here, as vegetation grows and dies, the top soil builds up. It compresses older layers of dead vegetation below, but its waterlogged nature inhibits decomposition. This is the process of peat formation. Being essentially compacted organic matter, peat will burn very well once it has been dried out. It is a cheap and convenient fuel for the people living in marshy landscapes, where sufficient wood may be hard to come by. As such, it is a resource that has been exploited across Europe for centuries, from the wetlands of eastern Europe to the fens of East Anglia in England, the bogs of Ireland and Scotland, and north to the cold coasts of Scandinavia. The peat is cut into blocks that are stacked in the sun, and when they are dry the 'bricks' can be thrown on open fires to keep homes warm through the winter. In truly wet regions, the holes left by the peat excavations slowly fill with water and new ponds form. In regions where peat extraction has been undertaken extensively, the landscape is peppered with these man-made bodies of water. Areas of sodden mire, once the nesting-ground of birds and the home of rare plants, are transformed into a mosaic of lakes with a new set of wildlife.

MAN-MADE FRESHWATER

A large carp lazes near the surface of a pool, leisurely sucking down insects from the water's surface. A tremendous splash shatters the peace and in the same instant sharp talons close with a vice-like grip across the back of the fish. The carp struggles frantically, but there is no escape; having appeared as if from nowhere, the white-tailed eagle now strains every muscle to hoist the heavy fish into the air. The commotion causes the other fish to scatter, but they soon regroup in a different corner of the pool. This wild-looking scene takes place in a man-made lake; specially excavated for the rearing of carp, it remains stocked full of these creatures and is a rich hunting-ground for the local eagles.

The presence of so many artificial ponds in Europe is evidence of the importance of fish as a food resource. Some fish-ponds, such as those in the Barycz Valley in south-west Poland, were dug back in the Middle Ages and have since developed into very rich ecosystems. Stocked with artificially high numbers of carp, other freshwater fish, and even crayfish (a type of freshwater lobster), they are home to a diversity of wildlife, but most particularly they are a paradise for fish-eaters (see box, p. 73: 'Crayfish'). Grebes nest in the reeds that fringe

The Eurasian Bittern

In that magical time when the dusky red light of the setting sun turns yellow into gold and brown into ruby, the marshes and reedbeds of Biebrza shine with glorious colour. Gentle winds rustle through the sun-dried sweet-grass and reed-mace, and a moustached warbler, perched precariously on a swaying stem, sings a gentle song, reminiscent of the nightingale.

Among the forest of sandy-coloured stalks skulks one of Europe's most secretive birds. So timid is this creature that it is rarely ever seen, but during the breeding season the bittern makes its presence known. The boom of a male bittern can be heard over 5km (3 miles) away and sometimes it will call every two seconds. The deep sound resonates across the reedbeds like the blast from a forlorn foghorn throughout the dusk and well into the night. The males are extremely aggressive as they defend their territories against intruding males and disputes may even result in fatalities. Owning a good territory means that a male can mate with several females which are attracted to the booming calls, and some polygamous males are known to have had as many as five females nesting in their territory.

Very occasionally a bittern will take flight. Airborne, on its rufous, rounded wings, it seems ponderous and slow. Flying low over the reedbeds, with legs trailing behind, a bittern looks like a cross between an owl and a heron. On the ground its appearance alters dramatically as it changes stance. Creeping stealthily through a forest of muddy reeds, stalking frogs and fish which feed among the roots, a bittern's progress is so slow that it seems each movement is calculated. Often a bittern will stand completely still and hunched up, like someone huddled in the cold, but its eyes are piercing and alert, on the lookout for the next tasty morsel to wander by. By contrast, when a bittern has been alarmed, perhaps by some strange rustle in nearby rushes, it will stand up straight and tall, head held erect and yellow-green bill pointing like a dagger towards the sky. This accentuates its plumage which, especially at the neck and chest, provides wonderful camouflage among the reeds and rushes, the bird being almost pin-striped in golden browns.

Despite its retiring nature the bittern was once a very common bird in Europe, but since the nineteenth century its numbers have dropped steadily in many countries. In these times of dramatic change, reedbeds and marshlands have suffered greatly. Whether drained for land reclamation or polluted by run-off from agriculture in the surrounding areas, good habitats have declined in number and size. Increased disturbance to reedbeds by boating and fishing is also thought to be much to blame for the decrease of this remarkable but very shy bird.

KJ

Crayfish

In the murky depths of a pond in central Europe, among the mud and rotting leaf litter, two sets of eyes twitch. Antennae flick like fly-fishing rods, wafting sediment in spinning plumes and delicately feeling the weeds and dead branches that lie on the pond bottom. Spidery legs, covered in sensitive hairs, probe the mulch beneath. Whiskery mouthparts beat a steady stream of water over chemically sensitive cells. It is autumn and this male crayfish is searching for a mate.

Crayfish are experts at hiding in the smallest nooks and crannies. It is thought that their name was derived long ago from 'crevice' or the French word, *crevasse* (crayfish translates into *écrevisse* in French, or *crevik* in Old Dutch). Females are found buried under leaf litter and stones so, as a male moves across the bottom of the pond, he investigates under leaves with his fine pincers. If a female moves beneath him, he pounces. Clasping her with his huge claws, he drags her from beneath the dead leaves and speedily begins to turn her with his finer walking legs. Their mouthparts beat ferociously as the two crayfish tumble in a flurry of snipping claws and ungainly legs. At first the female struggles but then, strangely, seems to fall into a faint and becomes limp and passive. Her claws stretch out above her head and the male quickly turns her on to her back. He covers her body, secreting sticky, white spermatophores – packages of sperm – on to her underside. When he has finished he wanders off in search off another mate but the female, as though stunned, remains prostrate for some time. She begins to produce little, blue-grey eggs that cluster on strands of sticky mucus beneath her abdomen. Her tail flap curls around them and the mucus forms a protective sheath between the end of her tail and her body, thus encasing the eggs. Fluid within the case dissolves the spermatophores and the sperm swim out to fertilize the eggs. The female can then forage across the bottom of the pond without losing her fertilized eggs. These will hatch in the early summer of the next year.

Crayfish are found throughout Europe in rivers, streams, canals and ponds. Some fish-ponds date from medieval times when carp and crayfish were an important food source for villages and towns. There are several distinct species of crayfish native to Europe, but they are now seriously threatened. Crayfish farming has become a huge industry and the gastronomic popularity of this crustacean may have led to its downfall. An American species, the signal crayfish, so-called because of the white flashes at the hinges of its claws, is very popular with farmers as it is larger, breeds faster and is tastier than the native European species. After being imported they often escape, or are illegally released into natural habitats.

Once in the wild, populations of signal, and other non-native, crayfish are almost impossible to eradicate. They spread quickly and cause severe environmental damage, burrowing extensively into river-banks, ripping out plants and preying on fish eggs and native crayfish. This alien species is not only more aggressive than the native crayfish but on its arrival in Europe brought with it a deadly fungal disease. Signal crayfish are mostly resistant to this 'plague' but whole colonies of native crayfish can be obliterated in days. It has already wiped out a great number of populations throughout Europe, and some species have been declared threatened or rare. Sadly, animal lovers may be endangering local indigenous populations. Signal crayfish, sold in pet shops as a curious alternative to goldfish, are master escape artists. They may find their way to habitats containing native populations, thus increasing the pressure on Europe's unique crayfish species.

AA/KJ

the ponds and otters play on the banks. Sometimes fish farmers may try and discourage furred and feathered thieves from their ponds, but generally the raiders are tolerated and even appreciated, both by the farmers and by groups of tourists who may visit to admire these wildlife oases.

Long before humans were digging holes to make ponds, beavers – Europe's largest rodents – were damming rivers throughout the continent to the same effect. However, the purpose of the pools they made was not to ensure a good supply of fish; beavers are strictly vegetarian. They create year-round deep water for two reasons: for storing food through the winter and to make certain that the underwater entrances to their lodges remain submerged. Beavers must feeds on twigs and bark during the winter, so in autumn they drag branches and small trees to the bottom of their ponds where the cold water preserves the bark's nutritional value. Their lodge is a large pile of sticks, stones and mud from which they gnaw out tunnels and chambers. Although the chambers are excavated above the surface level of the water, the entrances to the lodge are always underwater to make sure the family inside is not disturbed by unwanted visitors. Being far happier in the water than on land, the beaver will dig channels from its pond into the surrounding marsh. These canals enable easy access to food supplies and facilitate the dragging of branches back to the lodge.

People have also found waterways to be convenient means of transport and travel – so much so that natural rivers have been straightened, widened and dredged to accommodate boats, and canals have been cut to link the rivers together. The lowlands of Europe are now criss-crossed by a network of channels along which boats ferry people and goods between inland regions and to and from the coast. The completion in 1992 of the Main-Danube Canal (or Europa Canal), which connects the Rhine to the Danube via one of the Rhine's tributaries, has made it possible for water-borne traffic to navigate 3,500km (2,175 miles) from the Atlantic to the Black Sea, right through the heart of Europe. The final leg of that journey is down the Sulina Canal that carves through the Danube Delta: one of Europe's last great wildernesses.

THE DELTA

As the mighty Danube approaches the western coast of the Black Sea it slackens its pace, causing much of the sediment washed out of the interior to settle here. With thousands of tonnes of earth and sand being deposited each year, numerous banks and islands have built up, splitting the great river into a myriad smaller channels that spread out over 5,000sq km (1,930sq miles) so creating the largest continuous wetland in Europe and the most extensive reedbeds in the world. Although sliced in two by a major shipping highway, the greater part of the delta is accessible only by small boat, and only when the water-levels permit passage. These waters are too vast and unpredictable to have ever been tamed.

The productivity here is immense. The expanse of warm shallow waters, rich in nutrients, is home to huge numbers of fish of forty-five different species. These in turn support a multitude of other creatures; aquatic dice snakes live here, and they can dive down and catch freshwater gobies in the murky water. They can be seen holding their heads above the waves as they swim out from the shore of a large lake. Then they drop their heads down under the water to catch a fish; a successful catch is indicated by the body of the snake rotating at the surface as it grapples to get a good hold of its slippery prey. The snakes are unable to swallow their catch in the water so they swim with them to the shore. Back on solid ground the fish are easier to handle and the snake slowly 'walks' the gobies into its distensible jaws.

European pond terrapins find the delta a perfect habitat. Along the backwaters, where lines of willows droop into the sluggish current blocked by rotting logs and filled with a thick tangle of aquatic vegetation, the terrapins clamber out of the water to rest. Up above them the trees are filled with all the clamour of a breeding colony of herons, egrets, ibises and cormorants. A mixed heronry, with all its bustle and din, characterizes the essence of the Danube Delta. Though home to a truly rich array of plants and animals, it is the birds that are most evidently abundant here. The delta is home to 4,000 pairs of pygmy cormorants (which constitutes 60 per cent of the European population) and also to Europe's largest population of glossy ibises, spoonbills, herons, little egrets, stilts and avocets. Perhaps most impressive of all are the 3,000 pairs of white pelicans (making up 70 per cent of the European population).

The pelicans nest on floating islands of matted vegetation that rise and fall with the changing water-level. This ensures that their eggs and chicks are never drowned by unseasonal floods. A breeding colony of pelicans is a rare sight, for they select locations that are virtually impossible to reach by foot or by boat. But each day the adults rise up on the morning thermals and glide out over the marsh. They congregate on the lakes and pools to fish. The sight of a flock of several hundred of these giant birds effortlessly drifting overhead is something that never fails to enthral the small number of tourists who visit this secluded corner of Europe. They travel here to experience the enormous wealth of birds and other wildlife that thrives in the delta.

The Danube Delta is, and always has been, a very special place for wildlife. It is impressive in its size, in its variety of aquatic habitats, and in the wealth of wildlife it supports. But it is perhaps most impressive of all in its survival. Created by one of Europe's greatest rivers, this vast and largely inaccessible wetland remains an unconquered wilderness and a refuge for wetland wildlife. At a time when most of the wild wetlands of Europe have been drained or otherwise tamed, the Danube Delta remains the realm of frogs and herons, terrapins and pelicans. It is a testament to the richness of the freshwater habitat.

JC

CHAPTER 4

GRASSLANDS: ANCIENT & MODERN

OLD AND NEW GRASSLANDS

Grasslands, both ancient and modern, stretch across Europe from the natural open steppes of the Ukraine to the swathes of pastureland and swaying cereal crops over the rest of the continent. A specialist community of plants and animals takes its chance to make a living in both natural and modified grasslands.

A sleek red-footed falcon hovers gracefully over a sea of ancient grassland in Europe's eastern limit, the Ukraine. It holds its position with incredible precision despite a gusty wind, as its piercing red eyes survey the land below for the slightest movement. Now, at the height of the summer, there is an abundance of riches: grasshoppers, frogs, lizards and butterflies thrive while summer lasts. The falcon stoops to snatch a grasshopper, one of the hundred or more needed each day to feed two hungry chicks.

In western Europe, a huge combine harvester rumbles through an enormous expanse of wheat. The crop stretches as far as the eye can see. This is Europe's new grassland. It is a place where wheat and barley are grown on a grand scale. These crops, the modern-day grasses, arose from thousands of years of selection and hybridization of natural grasses by humans hungry for a reliable source of food. Today, cereal crops make up 70 per

Above

Przewalski's horses, a wild Asian race, graze the ancient grasslands of the Ukrainian steppe.

Opposite

A harvest mouse living in a wheat field, one of Europe's new grasslands.

Inset

Vast combine harvesters march across huge modern wheat fields.

cent of the world's harvested crops, a vital source of nutrition for humans, but how well can falcons and other grassland creatures like the harvest mouse fare here? This is the story of how grassland landscapes came to exist naturally, or were created by people for pastureland or for harvesting grain, and how grassland wildlife has taken advantage of the new openings with varying degrees of success.

THE UKRAINIAN STEPPE

In the far eastern corner of Europe, the Ukraine, where the continent meets Asia, lies a very special landscape. Grass ripples as far as the eye can see in an unbroken vista of steppe, the only place in the whole of Europe where this habitat occurs naturally. Steppe grassland is the equivalent of the North American prairie, or the savannah of Africa; the land is largely bereft of trees which need more rainfall, but not dry enough to become desert. The conditions for such grassland to form naturally are rare in Europe, and its survival is precarious: if the Ukrainian steppe received less than 25cm (10in) of rainfall per year it would desiccate and become too arid for grass to survive, while more than 100cm (40in) of rainfall each year would enable trees to take hold and, before long, the steppe would resemble the wooded landscapes that once covered most of the continent. Where natural steppe did develop, it became the home of a range of specialized grassland mammals and birds found nowhere else in Europe.

Askania Nova is a protected area, and part of the remaining Ukrainian steppe, where natural grasses blow in the wind across a vast horizon. Over huge areas there are no trees to provide shelter. Indeed, the only features are tall stone figures, built some 900 years ago, uncannily reminiscent of the local steppe marmots, or bobaks, sitting on their haunches and surveying the plains in their characteristic way. The stones face east and are thought to have acted as markers for the caravans of Asian nomads which passed over these steppes on their way west, to Europe. On the featureless plain, these markers must have been a vital navigational tool. The corridor of grassland provided by the steppes has been a regular route for invaders to Europe from the East over the millennia, including the Mongols of central Asia, and the Huns, who passed through on their way to conquer Hungary and lands further to the west. Grassland may have proved easier to move through than the woodlands to the north, but the migration of peoples through these areas may well reflect the importance of grass itself to them. Grass was not just vital to the wild creatures which thrived on it; it also provided food for domestic animals such as cattle, sheep and horses. The nomadic races relied on their domesticated animals for food and transport, and would have been attracted to grassy areas where their animals could feed.

Grass has a number of special properties that make it the ideal food for grazing animals, and which make grasslands ideal homes for many more. Grass often appears simply as a mass of small green leaves, but in fact it is a flowering plant, albeit with tiny flowers, which disperse pollen to the winds from the tops of spindly stems. Their seeds are often carried by wind, too, although many can hook on to the coats of passing animals for transport. But grasses do not rely totally on seeds to disperse; they have a huge ability to spread across open ground, using a network of horizontal runners capable of sending up new shoots. This network of roots binds soil together, often deep into the ground. As well as preventing erosion, this creates ideal conditions for a host of burrowing animals to make their homes.

Grass is also incredibly resilient to drought, burning, freezing and flooding, and survives where trees could never cope, but it is its resilience in another way which is the key to how it supports so many specialist animals. If a blade of grass is cut or grazed, it continues to grow –

just like a human hair. Unlike most plants, grass grows not from the tip but from nodes in the stem, some of them in a crucial position at the base of the plant near the soil, enabling it to survive even heavy grazing remarkably well. Around the world, large communities of grazing animals have evolved to exploit this wonder plant, which recovers time and time again from their attentions. Grass actually relies on grazers for its survival in many places. In areas where bushes and trees could survive the climate, grazers stop their spread by nipping their growth in the bud before they become established and shade out the grass.

In Askania Nova some of the original European grass-eating mammals still survive. A female steppe marmot, a hare-sized member of the squirrel family for whom the Ukraine is the only European toe-hold, stands erect on her metre-high nest mound, the highest vantage point in this flat landscape. Her teats are swollen with milk, and she scans the horizon for possible dangers; a brief whistle in response to spotting a steppe eagle would bring her young racing back to the burrow. After ten weeks underground, they are getting their first glimpses of daylight, and cannot afford to stray far from their mother's side. Soon they will be weaned, and will start to graze the juicy fresh grass alongside her.

Many smaller mammals thrive here too; steppe voles, long-tailed field mice and common and grey hamsters live in countless burrows, while tiny harvest mice weave delicate nests up among the grasses. Wild flowers such as dwarf irises and tulips abound, providing a riot of colour. These and many other steppe plants sprout each spring from bulbs and rhizomes which survive from year to year in the undisturbed soil of the plains. Insects abound on the flowers, and graze on the profusion of vegetation. Many kinds of grasshoppers live here as well, and two resident species of locust are occasionally joined by swarms of migratory locusts from Asia, which in turn are followed by flocks of rose-coloured starlings that track the locusts' movements and gorge on these insects.

Ground-nesting birds such as stone curlews and skylarks find plenty of cover for their nests, while some birds actually benefit from the burrowing activities of mammals. Shelducks search the grasslands for underground homes in which to lay their eggs, and abandoned marmot burrows are perfect. The shelducks are no threat to the marmots, who can keep possession of burrows they are still using, but another creature, a snake rustling through the grass, causes panic all round. The marmot shakes her whole body and whistles to her young. A male skylark rises and sings loudly over the steppe, thereby attempting to distract the threat away from his camouflaged mate on her nest. A steppe vole runs to the safety of its burrow as an Orsini's viper slithers among the roots.

This small but venomous snake is a real threat to voles, although much of its diet is actually insects. In the spring, however, male snakes are often searching not for food but for mates. When the male finds a female curled up in the tall grass, he begins the process of seduction by sidling up to her and wrapping himself around her body. This is the beginning of a remarkable reptilian spectacle. Before long, a second male arrives, then another and another, and a writhing mass of vipers soon gathers in the grass. Eventually, just one male succeeds in mating with the female, and the rest slither off to seek other mates.

The great steppes of the Ukraine were once home to a range of large mammalian grazers. Red and roe deer are still common, while Europe's only antelope, the saiga, which was once hunted almost to extinction, is protected here, and its numbers have recovered amazingly fast thanks to its remarkable breeding rate. This animal looks nothing like the graceful antelopes of Africa. It is more like a strange sheep, with rather short legs and a distinctive swollen snout, as if it has come off worst in a violent boxing match. Its odd look, however, reflects how well it has adapted to the demands of the steppe. In the dry summer, large numbers on the move

Above
*Wild tulips are
common in the
Ukrainian steppe,
their bulbs surviving
from year to year in
the undisturbed soil.*

kick up huge clouds of dust, but their noses now play their part, filtering out the dust with special membranes that line convoluted internal bones. The Ukraine saiga once stayed on the move for much of the year, as saiga herds still do further to the east in the Asian steppes, travelling further south for the winter, and moving back north as conditions warm in the spring. Steppe conditions, however, are very unpredictable, and the herds are constantly on the move, avoiding poor weather and seeking good grazing. New arrivals have to be capable of joining the migrating herd within only a day or so of birth, to avoid being left behind.

Przewalski's horses – a wild race from Asia – also graze on the herb-rich grasses of the Ukrainian steppe, enjoying the protection afforded to them by the park authorities of Askania Nova, having narrowly avoided extinction in the 1960s. The local race of wild horse, the tarpan, survived until the second half of the last century, when the last of its race was killed in the Ukraine. European bison once lived here too, but today have only survived in Europe thanks to the protection they receive in the great Białowieża forest of Poland, which is now a national park (see box, p. 57: 'European Bison'). The now extinct great wild ox or aurochs, grazed here until some 2,000–3,000 years ago, before being hunted to extinction. However, they have left descendants in the form of domestic cattle.

It is hard to pinpoint exactly where cattle, horses, sheep and goats were first domesticated, and the process probably happened in a number of places in the Middle East, Asia and Europe at various times. What is certain, however, is that the people who came to live on the great steppes some 8,000–10,000 years ago soon came to rely on domesticated grazing animals for food and clothing, and the horse became an important means of transport. Where pastureland did not exist, they created new grasslands, and not just on the fringes of the original steppe. Over the last 10,000 years there has been a generally westward migration of people accompanied by domestic animals into Europe. These nomadic pastoralists took over land where small populations of humans were eking out a living by hunting mainly forest animals, and collecting food from wild plants. The migrating herders created further open pastureland for their livestock to graze by clearing forests as they went. Grass sprang up quickly in the new clearings and, as long as the newly opened landscape was grazed consistently, the forests were prevented from regenerating and grassland established itself. Such clearance of woodland to be replaced by grass has influenced landscapes all over Europe, especially in the west where few grasslands existed naturally.

Europe can be viewed as a large peninsula protruding from the western edge of Asia. The climate varies hugely across the continent, depending on elevation, distance from the sea and a host of other factors, and strongly affects which kinds of plants can grow where. Without our influence, western Europe, with its wet and mild maritime climate, would naturally be largely covered in mixed deciduous woodland. Only further east, in the Ukraine and beyond, does the dryness of the climate and the far greater range of temperatures between summer and winter favour grass as the dominant vegetation. The huge areas of lowland grasslands found elsewhere in Europe today have been created by us.

THE HORTOBÁGY

Moving west from the Ukraine, vast expanses of grassland, or *puszta* as it is called locally, are now found in the Hortobágy, a region comprising some 10,000sq km (3,860sq miles) of the great Hungarian plain. This is a classic example of an apparently natural habitat which has been largely created by humans. The natural and domestic fauna, along with the local human culture, all reflect the region's history. Today, the horse, one of the animals which accompanied the first settlers here, still plays a vital role on this area. Traditional horsemen or *csikós*, dressed in a style dating back centuries and with blue pleated sleeves billowing in the wind, can still be seen cracking long whips above their heads in the still air as they drive herds of Nonius horses to watering holes twice each day. Wide-brimmed hats, adorned with bustard feathers, provide protection from the hot sun. The horsemen must draw water by hand from hundred-year-old

Below

Vast numbers of grasshoppers graze Europe's grasslands and fall prey to steppe tarantulas and red-footed falcons.

wells, to keep their livestock from becoming parched. The once prolific Nonius breed, a cross between local horses and those brought from Normandy in the Napoleonic wars, has now declined to a mere 600 individuals, but their prospects are now improving.

The Hortobágy's first settlers would have found a habitat very different to today's open plain. The landscape is thought to have been originally a mosaic of marshland, wet grassland, wooded areas and natural clearings in the loops of the mighty River Tisza, a tributary of the Danube. Each year the Tisza burst its banks and covered the flood plain with rich silt, a fantastic boost to fertility. Some areas were permanently inundated as the river was unregulated, but since the mid-nineteenth century it has been prevented from flooding by huge dams and extensive dykes. Grand oaks, and other trees, once grew along the marshy river-banks and provided nest sites for white storks which hunted frogs and other amphibians in the damp grasslands. Although rare, this situation still exists today in a few places in Europe, such as the flood plains of the great Danube river in Austria, but no longer in the Hortobágy. Wild horses and aurochs used to graze the natural woodland clearings, but they have been gradually replaced by domestic herds as the Hortobágy was cleared and populated. Some oak and willow forests persisted in lowland areas, but the central part of the plain eventually became open grassland as the land dried out and the last woods, which needed the moisture, were unable to regenerate.

Although the Hungarian *puszta* was largely created by humans, and grazed by domestic animals, many of the wild inhabitants of the natural steppes to the east moved in as it was opened up, and live there to this day. First impressions of one such immigrant can be unforgettable: in the early morning spring mists, a hard-to-define shape moves across the horizon. The featureless grassland makes it difficult to be sure of distance and size. Could it be a roe deer, a large bird, or perhaps just a floating plastic bag? Closer inspection with binoculars reveals the proudly strutting shape of a male great bustard at the peak of his annual courtship display. Chestnut wings, turned inside out, reveal a ball of white under-feathers. Beneath the erect tail is an extravagant ruff of feathers. A white, wispy moustache falls lightly over grey stripes running down each side of his hugely puffed-out neck. Female great bustards wander by in small bands, apparently unimpressed by the male's elaborate display. Eventually, when a male reaches the height of his sexual frenzy a female may begin to pay him some attention, but it might take several weeks of display before a male is accepted as a mate (see box, p. 84: 'Great Bustards').

To protect the great bustard, and a wide range of other specialist grassland wildlife, the Hortobágy National Park was established in 1972. In the natural Ukrainian steppe, occasional stands of trees act as magnets to all sorts of birds, since they provide the only nest sites for many species, including red-footed falcons. Primarily to attract these rare falcons, the Hortobágy National Park has planted stands of black locust trees, whose deep tap roots can reach the lowered water-table. The scheme has been a great success.

Rooks were among the first to move in, and their presence has been the key to attracting falcons. The bulky, jet-black rooks are frequently seen strolling confidently through the grass like smartly besuited gentlemen, picking over the soil for insect grubs and worms, before carrying food back to their chicks. Their noisy, crowded tree-top colonies, with large untidy nests of loosely assembled twigs and sticks standing out clearly against the sky, have proven to be a magnet for the falcons; the new building developments on the *puszta* have rapidly become prized real estate, and as the rooks feed their young, the sharp-eyed red-footed falcons circle over the colony.

The falcons have migrated north from Africa to breed in Europe. In Hungary, they find plenty of juicy grasshoppers, their staple diet, and now they also find ready-made nests. Slate grey males, their silvery flight feathers catching the light as they turn, perform aerial courtship displays for the rusty-coloured females. Below, the rooks take flight and rasp out warnings to defend their space. The courting falcons boldly land in a rook's nest, but a single dive-bomb by a rook is enough to send them on their way; they can always return later. For now, they turn their attention to mating, a brief affair for these birds, performed while balancing precariously on a locust tree branch under the watchful gaze of the nesting rooks. The falcons are effectively staking this nest out, and as soon as the young rooks have fledged the falcons will move in to lay their eggs. Like the rooks, red-footed falcons breed in colonies, and as many as ten pairs now nest in clumps of trees in the park. They have also started to take over old magpie nests, which are found in many trees growing alongside roads through the *puszta*.

Within sight of the rook colony, a flock of odd-looking sheep with remarkable corkscrew horns grazes. Long before the park was established, herds of domestic cattle and sheep played a major part in keeping this semi-natural grassland free from scrub and trees. The park now keeps the spread of such vegetation at bay with a range of ancient breeds for which the area is famous, but which were on the decline. Racka sheep closely resemble sheep depicted in both Mesopotamian and Egyptian paintings, with laterally protruding, twisted horns, and may represent one of the oldest breeds, probably descended from Asian wild sheep. During the summer, the Racka sheep roam far and wide to find the most succulent areas on which to feed. They are followed by large flocks of starlings, which eat the insects flushed out by the sheep's trampling feet.

Herds of Hungarian grey cattle are also preserved here. These enormous beasts with majestic, upright horns, and a pale grey coat, are quite unlike most modern breeds of cattle, and are thought by some to have been domesticated in this part of Europe from the wild aurochs. They are brought by the herdsmen to traditional hand-drawn wells to drink water drawn from great depths beneath the plain.

As summer continues, the grass on the *puszta* dries up, becoming parched and yellow. The young rooks have fledged and join the adults in huge flocks wheeling over the *puszta*; back at the rookery, the only remaining sign of the rooks are their abandoned nests and a few black feathers scattered over the ground. The young red-footed falcons have just hatched and will be in the nest for four weeks. In the heat of high summer, the adult red-footed falcons work hard to provide food for their hungry young, hovering over the dry plain in their search for insects. Grasshoppers are well camouflaged, brown on brown, yellow on yellow, green on green, but the slightest movement betrays their presence to the falcons, which swoop down to snatch them with their grasping talons.

Even if they escape the hovering falcons, the grasshoppers must contend with another predator, this time on the ground, or rather under it. Europe's largest spider, the steppe tarantula, which spans 6cm (2½in) from the tip of its hairy front feet to the tips of its hairy back feet, waits in its burrow for a hint of movement above ground. The grasshopper's camouflage is no defence against this alert predator, which tunes into the slightest vibrations in the earth and along the strands of silk that form a delicate apron around the burrow entrance. As a grasshopper moves carefully through the grass, on its way to lay eggs in the warm soil, it is quite unaware that the spider is lying in wait nearby. As the grasshopper edges too close, the spider strikes, leaping forward to subdue the insect in its large poison fangs, before retreating to its burrow to suck out the juices.

Other burrows conceal creatures rather more attractive to most people than the tarantulas: sousliks, Europe's only ground squirrels. These little creatures expanded their

Great Bustards

On a vast, flat plain a grasshopper munches a blade of grass, unaware that it is being stalked. Cautiously, a very large bird moves forward on carefully placed, dark-olive feet. With a quick snap, the grasshopper is plucked from the grass stem. Dashing the insect against the ground, the great bustard turns it in its bill and quickly swallows it.

The great bustard, standing at around 90cm (36in) tall, is one of the largest land birds in Europe. It is a bird of the open grassland and steppe but is also adapted to living in some crop fields. The range of the great bustard has been greatly affected by humans throughout history; sadly, today its numbers are dwindling and there is cause for concern.

Bustards are very gregarious and forage through the grasses in huge groups, or 'droves', usually of the same sex or age. They are very wary birds and are said to need at least 1km (½ mile) of open land on three sides at any one time in order to feel secure. As some of the group stalk through the grass, heads low, carefully inspecting the ground for their prey, others stand tall, keeping a sharp eye on the horizon for predators. Their camouflaging colours serve them well in the grass, but if surprised by a predator, they shoot up in the air on powerful wings. Despite their huge size, great bustards are incredibly swift in flight.

As humans spread across Europe, felling forests to cultivate crops such as rape and kale, they created some ideal habitats for the great bustards whose numbers and range spread as the landscape opened up before them. As their habitats increased, so too did their numbers. At the end of the eighteenth century, when forest clearance had reached its full extent across Europe, their populations had never been greater. Moving in vast droves of over a thousand birds, the great bustard flourished with the changes that humans had brought to the landscape – but it was a short-lived triumph. Agricultural practices changed; mosaics of rough grassland and small crop fields, ideal habitats for the birds, were swallowed up by intensively farmed monocultures. Crop fields ceased to be quiet, insect-rich havens bordered by natural steppe, becoming instead highly managed with pest-control sprays, irrigation and huge machines. The birds were also hunted for their meat and, unable to live with such disturbances, their numbers plummeted. Throughout the nineteenth century local populations were wiped out and the once massive range of this bird shrank to tiny fragmented groups. With the continuing modernization of agricultural practices they are still very much threatened and their numbers continue to fall at an alarming rate.

One of the most internationally important populations of great bustard exists in Spain. Here there may be as many as 12,000 birds, but their numbers are fragmented into isolated groups of, in some places, only 15 birds. Studies are under way to assess the effects of this on the population as a whole. To the east, on the great Hungarian plain, around 1,000 birds still breed. Here the great bustard is regarded as a national symbol. To kill one of these magnificent birds would incur a fine of nearly sixteen times the average annual wage in Hungary. However, if the bird is to survive it needs a habitat in which it can live – an open, quiet plain, without disturbance. Bustards exist in a fragment of their former territory, and with increasing pressures for more crops and faster production perhaps even these last domains may one day simply be history.

KJ

Opposite
A traditional horseman, or csikó, *dressed in a centuries-old style, drives his Nonius horses across the Hungarian* puszta.

Opposite inset
Racka sheep, an ancient race, probably descended from Asian wild sheep, graze in the Hortobágy National Park.

range from their strongholds to the east, and from small populations on higher ground, into Hungary's new grasslands as they were created. During the summer months, these engaging little animals feast on all the grass they can eat, and gather more to take down their burrows for winter food and bedding. If a bird of prey, such as a marsh harrier or black kite (for whom the souslik is a favourite prey item), flies over, the sousliks give shrill alarm calls warning others of danger, prompting a swift retreat underground (see box, p. 86: 'The Souslik').

The grasslands are not the only places to find wildlife in the Hortobágy. Storks nest on the telegraph poles lining the main road in the village of Nagyvan. Here, telegraph poles are more common than trees, and to encourage the stork population not to nest on chimneys the telephone company has built platforms on which the storks can breed. The storks feed their hungry broods, while below them villagers cycle by on their way home from the fields. Chickens run around a farmyard while a farmer grinds last autumn's maize to provide food for his animals. These days, the grazing of domestic animals is not the only form of farming in this area. Another great human innovation, again based on the remarkable properties of grass, is becoming more important in this area: the growing of cereal crops. The domestication of wild grasses to create agricultural cereals has fuelled the spread of human civilization and transformed the landscape more than anything else.

The Souslik

In the light of the mid-morning sun, the flat grassy plain is curiously quiet and still. The sun-warmed ground is pocked with holes, the entrances to many tunnels. A large shadow is cast over one of them as a steppe eagle waits and, with determined patience, studies the entrance. Minutes earlier the eagle had swept down on to the plain but was spotted by the keen eye of an alert souslik. Whistling a high-pitched call, the rodent warned other feeding sousliks of the eagle's anticipated attack. In seconds, the fast-moving animals dashed into the safety of their burrows.

The souslik is well known for this alarm signal and is sometimes called the 'whistler'. Sousliks, a type of ground squirrel, are well adapted to life on the plains; their smooth, slightly mottled, honey-coloured fur serves well to camouflage them in the golden grasses. Their dark eyes, accentuated by a lid-lining of soft white fur, sit high on their head – all the better for watching for predators. They have slim but very strong bodies and short legs, ideal for digging down into the ground and moving quickly through tunnels.

Sousliks live in vast colonies, but each has its own burrow. Their numbers can be immense. In an area of around 334sq m (3,674sq ft) there can be as many as 12,000 burrow entrances. Adults usually have two burrows, also called dens or lodges. The main lodge is more extensive, the second a retreat for emergencies, but both have two entrances that are constantly surrounded by fresh piles of excavated soil. The sousliks make alterations to their dens every day – extending side tunnels, digging latrine chambers and, if pregnant, females will prepare a grass-lined nesting chamber.

In March the sousliks awaken from a seven-month hibernation. First the males emerge, and three weeks later the females join them. Only days after the females have woken up the males, squeaking loudly, begin chasing them across the grasslands, and eventually are rewarded with a mating. Just under a month later the females give birth to about six naked, helpless babies. It is another month before the young emerge from their mothers' dens but they immediately begin an independent life, digging their burrows and living in them.

As the first farmers spread across the European landscapes they felled extensive areas of forest and created more and more grassland and crop fields. This was ideal habitat for the sousliks, which spread west with the changing landscape, greatly extending their range. However, more recent changes in agricultural practices have been detrimental to many populations of souslik. Their numbers and ranges have been greatly reduced in many areas. Where they do exist they can cause a great deal of damage to crops and are often regarded as pests by farmers. But sousliks, and other burrowing animals, have an essential role on the plains. By digging into the ground and pushing their excavations to the surface they churn and turn the soil, and by carrying nesting materials down into their chambers and using latrines there they transfer rich organic materials below the windswept ground. This mixing of the surface soils and organic materials helps to maintain the nutrient richness of the plains and so the healthy growth of grasses.

Sousliks also have another important role on the plains. At a burrow entrance a nose appears. The souslik sniffs the air cautiously and its whiskers twitch. It edges further out, eyes wide and muscles tensed, ready to dash back to safety at the slightest hint of danger. The grass nearby is lush and the souslik is hungry. It has waited for some time in its burrow and perhaps now it is safe to emerge. The decision is made and the souslik moves forward out of the shelter of its den. Too late, it suddenly sees movement as the steppe eagle jumps forward. Sharp talons catch the squealing animal, and the eagle bites at the struggling souslik with its strong beak. The little rodent will make a good meal for the steppe eagles' young chicks which, still some way from fledging, need all the nourishment they can get. The eagle takes off, carrying her prey over the grasslands.

KJ

For millennia, even before the advent of settled agriculture, grass seeds were an important human food. Today, 70 per cent of all harvested crops are classified as grasses, although some bear little resemblance to the natural grasses from which they are descended. Wheat, barley, rice and maize are now staples in Europe. Wheat and barley were the first grasses to be domesticated in the world, and this took place in the Fertile Crescent, the area that is now northern Israel, northern Syria and Iraq, some 10,000 years ago. They have since spread westwards throughout Europe. The other main cereals of the world were domesticated relatively recently: rice from wild rice around 8,000 years ago in China, and maize some 5,000 years ago from the wild grass, teosinte, in Mexico.

Towards the end of the last Ice Age, 12–13,000 years ago, certain large-seeded grasses grew in the hills of the Fertile Crescent. They seem to have become a regular part of the diet of hunter–gatherers, who collected, stored and ate the wild grain for thousands of years before they learned to cultivate it. This most important 'super-grass', emmer wheat, appears to have arisen by chance as a natural cross between two wild grasses, wild einkorn and wild goat grass. The resulting hybrid then doubled its chromosome number to become a viable new species.

It is thought that the hunter–gatherers may first have learned to scatter some of the seeds, or grain, of these grasses to encourage the plants' growth, and then to spread them beyond their natural habitat to grow the first crops. Emmer wheat was widely cultivated in the Neolithic period, some 8,000 years ago, and spread rapidly throughout central Europe, reaching north-west Europe and Britain by 6,000 years ago. Wheat was perfect for cultivating, since it not only had larger grains than other wild grasses, but also a stronger stem and tougher seed heads which did not shatter on ripening and thus retained the grains until they were harvested. Several new varieties of wheat emerged over the succeeding millennia; these included durum wheat, the basis of pasta making, and bread wheat. The latter largely replaced emmer during the Iron Age, around 2,000 years ago, and it is this crop which has been improved and developed, particularly in the last 300 years, to give the modern bread wheat on which we rely so heavily today.

The planting of cereal and other crops has increased rapidly in the *puszta* in the last sixty years, and around the edge of the Hortobágy National Park, men and horses now work the land together. Some farmers have reverted to traditional methods of agriculture since the communist cooperatives of which they were part were disbanded around a decade ago. Under communism, farmers' cooperatives had access to state-owned tractors, combine harvesters, pesticides and herbicides. This was good for guaranteeing plentiful crops, but not so beneficial for wildlife. Where heavy machinery once rumbled by, a farmer and his horse now labour to pull a heavy plough through the hard soil. Mammals and birds in their path have plenty of time to scramble to safety. The reprieve may only be temporary as some farmers much prefer the use of mechanical beasts, rather than relying on living ones. Some families have chosen to sell their land to local businessmen who have the resources to buy in mechanization in the form of irrigators and combine harvesters. Today the area's main roads are used by horse-drawn carts and heavy lorries alike.

Once autumn arrives, and temperatures drop, life on the grasslands changes. The red-footed falcons head back towards Africa from August onwards, and the sousliks spend less and less time above ground. By late October they are all curled up in their burrows ready to hibernate, only emerging in March when the spring sunshine lifts the gloom of winter. Humans also collect and store grass for the winter. In late summer, hay is cut and piled high on the back of horse-drawn carts and then stored in hayricks to provide food for the horses, cattle and sheep over the long, cold winter. Far from the influence of the Atlantic Ocean with its warming Gulf Stream, winter temperatures regularly remain far below zero for several months.

Above left

Some farmers in eastern Hungary have reverted to using horse-drawn ploughs since the fall of communism.

Above right

Yellowhammers nesting in a traditional English hedgerow.

During the golden days of autumn the maize grown on the edge of the national park is harvested. Some fields are full of spilled grain, left there especially to encourage some very special visitors. Huge flocks of migrating cranes gather in the Hortobágy to refuel on this bounty before continuing their long journey from northern Europe to North Africa and the Near East. Tens of thousands of cranes need somewhere to roost and feed along the way, and the Hortobágy has become one of their most important stopover sites. Huge fish ponds, adjacent to the park, are drained for the fish harvest and then refilled to a level perfect for the roosting cranes. Against the setting sun, after a day's feeding on maize, they prepare to sleep in a haven provided for them in a grassland created by humans.

GRASSLANDS FURTHER WEST

The pattern that exists today in Hungary, where the population relies on a mixture of pastoralism and growing of cereals, has spread further west, right across Europe, and in the last 2,000 years most of the former forests of western Europe have been cleared. Agricultural land now accounts for more than 42 per cent of the total land area of Europe, although the proportion varies from less than 10 per cent in Finland, Sweden and Norway (where vast coniferous forests still cloak the land) to 70 per cent or more in the UK, the Ukraine, Hungary and Ireland. Farming has shaped much of Europe's landscape and has had a fundamental impact on the wild animals of the continent, for many of whom agricultural landscapes are now home. Like any other habitat, the number of openings it offers to different plants and animals depends on how varied it is.

As shifting cultivators took up settled agriculture, they created permanent fields which were often delineated by lines of uncut trees; these became known as hedgerows. Grazing by domestic animals remained important alongside the growing of crops. In the UK, large areas of the countryside were often left as common grazing land, providing food for the community's herds of sheep and cattle. During the sixteenth century, however, the enclosures movement began. Large areas of common grazing land were divided up to create small fields bounded by fast-growing hawthorn, and many of today's hedgerows date back to this period. By the mid-eighteenth century the pattern was largely complete. The hedges at once mark boundaries, prevent livestock from wandering, act as windshields for crops and shelters for animals, and as useful sources of wood for people. Every hedgerow is a miniature woodland, and the oldest and most diverse hedges generally have the most wildlife. You can estimate the approximate age of a hedgerow by counting the number of different shrub species, such as hawthorn, hazel, spindle and elder, growing in each 30m (99ft) length, and multiply by a hundred years for each species counted.

In today's more open farmland, hedgerows act as refuges for species once common in former woodland. The hedgehog, which takes its name from this habitat, can usually be found sleeping under hedges by day. It is here that they often rear their litter, suckling them at first, until the young are old enough to follow their mother in snuffling through the undergrowth in search of slugs, beetles, worms and other small prey. Foxes, too, frequently make their homes here, excavating their earths in the soil under hedgerow roots. At night, hedgehogs venture out into the open; pastureland is perhaps their favourite hunting ground, with lots of worms and beetle grubs to dig for.

The badger shares a very similar diet, and reaches its highest densities where large areas of open pastureland are available, as long as clumps of woodland remain where they can dig their setts. Badgers and hedgehogs, however, are rarely found in numbers in the same areas, and it's not just because their diets overlap so much. Badgers are voracious predators of hedgehogs, and one of the few animals that can cope with the hedgehog's classic defence of rolling up into a spiny ball: the badgers simply unroll them with their tough claws, and attack their soft underbellies. Not surprisingly, if hedgehogs get a whiff of badgers or their droppings, they leave the area rapidly.

Hidden in the long grass at the foot of the hedge a pair of yellowhammers feed their young. The nest, made of dried grasses with a fine grass lining, goes almost unnoticed, only given away by the toings and froings of the adults. Since the very start of spring the male's distinctive song, a 'chi-chi-chi-chi-chi . . . chwee', has been drifting across the fields from the top of the hedgerows. These birds are seed-eaters for most of the year, although the young are fed on insects, especially caterpillars. After twelve days the first brood are learning to fly, and soon the parents are preparing for a second egg-laying session. Once all the young have been raised, the yellowhammers come together and large flocks can be seen searching stubble fields for grain left after the harvest. Yellowhammers are just one of a number of birds which frequently nest in hedges: song thrushes, blackbirds, robins and various kinds of finch and warbler. But in much of western Europe, many of these birds have declined sharply in numbers over the last fifty years, as the whole process of farming has become more mechanized, more reliant on pesticides and herbicides, and grander in scale (see box, p. 94: 'The Decline of Farmland Birds').

AGRICULTURE AND THE FUTURE

Agricultural advances have helped ensure the supply of food for us, but in recent decades the cost of the changes they have brought to the landscape and its inhabitants has become all too clear: pollution of water sources by pesticides and herbicides, depletion of vital trace elements in soils and thus our diets, rural unemployment and depopulation, and perhaps most noticeable of all, the radical change in the way agricultural land looks. Many hedges have been cleared throughout north-western Europe, and the former patchwork of small fields, each growing a different crop, or alternating grazing land with planted land, has often given way to huge fields growing similar crops.

The urge to create larger and larger fields has partly been driven by the development of ever bigger agricultural machinery, designed to cut down the time taken to work the land. Enormous combine harvesters efficiently cut swathes through acres of wheat, leaving very little grain on which yellowhammers and other birds can feed. Many of the former inhabitants of farmlands are no longer able to make a living here. Some birds, along with hedgehogs, have found new homes in the increasingly leafy suburban gardens of our towns; a well-kept herbaceous border can provide a more varied diet for birds and hedgehogs than acres of sterile croplands and the occasional over-sprayed, mechanically cut hedgerow. These huge open fields, protected by fewer and fewer hedges, now suffer far greater loss of topsoil, which simply blows away in dry weather. In the long-term, large-scale agriculture may not prove so cost-effective after all.

Some animals that did manage to make a home for themselves in the wheat fields, rather than just around the margins, are also suffering increasingly. The harvest mouse, once a denizen of natural grassland, moved into planted wheat fields readily. It is the smallest European mouse, and the only one with a prehensile tail for gripping grass stems. The strong stems of modern wheat plants provided a sturdy foundation for the harvest mouse's neat spherical nest, which it was able to weave from wheat leaves to house its young. The wheat itself provided a plentiful supply of food, and for centuries, during which the wheat was cut by hand, the harvest mouse raised its young in relative safety. Today, combine harvesters cut the wheat earlier in the season than ever before as shorter crop rotations are practised, and the harvest mouse's days in the modern wheat fields are numbered, as combines regularly mow down the nests of harvest mice before the young are ready to leave. The adults may escape, but many young are lost to the harvester's mechanized jaws.

Wide-scale impoverishment of the countryside by modern forms of agriculture is becoming increasingly apparent. Does the productivity it has brought justify the damage? In Western Europe, total agricultural production has increased significantly since the 1950s, and grain, meat and other food shortages have become a thing of the past. But in the European Union (EU), increases in production have actually produced an excess of supply in some sectors, giving rise to wine lakes and mountains of butter and grain. One of the main beneficiaries of this excess has been the brown rat, along with a range of grain weevils, which usually find a way to feast on stored grain, however carefully it is kept. At night, rats regularly find a way into the modern fortresses that are grain silos and chew their way through what would otherwise become our daily bread. These animals came to Europe from Asia early in the eighteenth century aboard trading vessels from Russia. They have since proliferated wherever we have developed farming communities, using their intelligence and agility to take advantage of our crops, both growing and stored.

Now, at the close of the twentieth century, the face of Europe looks set to change once again as political systems are being revolutionized, and fresh approaches to land management are tried out. Communism has fallen in most Eastern European states. The USSR has disbanded and Comecon, the economic union of communist states, died in the late 1980s. Now, many Eastern European countries are keen to join the European Union and, particularly, to be included in its Common Agricultural Policy (CAP) which, until its reform in 1992, guaranteed high prices for the unlimited production of food. This gave a great boost to farmers, but was bad news for wildlife.

In the mid 1980s, the EU acknowledged that agriculture had a significant and detrimental effect on the environment, and that overproductivity needed curbing. By 1992, member states were compelled to make payments to farmers who set aside, or left out of production, some of their land within 'Environmentally Sensitive Areas' affected by agriculture. Many believe that the CAP remains unsustainable in both economic and environmental terms, and EU agricultural policy is once again being reviewed. It remains to be seen whether the EU's new agricultural policies will benefit wildlife, but either way, modern farming methods look set to remain a major influence on landscapes and their inhabitants for some time to come. In the meantime, a combination of set-aside land and a range of conservation schemes is helping some species.

Set-aside areas are potentially a haven for wildlife. In the UK, the Royal Society for the Protection of Birds (RSPB), reports that, on average, four times more birds are found on set-aside land than on other areas of farmland. The value of set-aside land for birds, however, depends crucially upon how that land is managed. Rules for the managing of set-aside land are complex, but the most bird-friendly set-asides would be a mixture of seasonally unfarmed and permanently unfarmed sites. The former provide stubble as a valuable winter feeding area, and the latter some open, undisturbed ground for ground nesting birds such as the skylark.

The RSPB has secured some exemptions from set-aside rules which enable farmers to manage land especially for birds such as the stone curlew and the lapwing. In the Scottish Hebrides and the Orkney Islands, hay cutting is being delayed and bird-friendly mowing techniques employed to protect the corncrake. The combine harvester works from the centre of the field first, working its way out towards the edge of the field in a spiral pattern, thus allowing these ground-nesting birds to escape with their lives. As a result, the corncrake population has increased by 20 per cent in the past two years on the islands. In the Netherlands, waders such as godwits and curlews nesting in wet grassland are being protected by volunteers who plant flags on sticks to indicate exactly where the nests are. The farmers can then avoid destroying the nests when they harvest the grass.

Much can also be done to provide food and shelter for animals even on the edges of intensively farmed fields. In the UK, the Game Conservancy has pioneered two methods of protecting game and other wildlife within the modern agricultural context. 'Conservation

Headland' and 'Beetle Bank' schemes are both viable options for farmers in Europe. A Conservation Headland is a metre-wide strip which is left unsprayed and unharvested at the edge of a cereal field. It provides nesting cover for birds and an unsprayed haven for insects and plants, which supply food for the birds and their offspring. Yellowhammers and skylarks thrive in such settings. Hedgerow wildlife also benefits from being further out of the range of pesticides and herbicides

Beetle Banks operate on a similar principle, providing havens for wildlife within an otherwise hostile environment. A bank of earth is created down the centre of an arable field and natural grasses planted to encourage a healthy population of beetles. These banks provide warm, undisturbed homes for beetles, and the beetles in turn act as pest-managers for the farmer in the wheat field. As the wheat begins to ripen and the population of aphids and other pests swells, ladybirds and various predatory beetles head out from the beetle banks into the crops and go to work, devouring many of the pests. The beetles act as a form of biological control on the pests, thus reducing the requirement for pesticides in these fields.

Some agricultural landscapes in Western Europe are more wildlife-friendly still. Some 'organic' farmers, who use no manufactured chemical products on their crops, would argue that their entire farms, rather than just metre-wide strips around the edge of each field, are conservation headlands. Although organic farming accounts for 0.5 per cent of European

Above

Red-footed falcons nesting in an old rook's nest. They, like kestrels, thrive in diverse grasslands where small prey abounds.

Opposite

A rich diversity of flowers growing in organically managed farmland.

The Decline of Farmland Birds

On a chilly, early spring morning, fluttering high in the blue sky, a male skylark broadcasts his song across the frosty fields below. He is trying to attract a mate. His burst of song ends as he flutters back down to his perch on a twig in the hedgerow that stretches between the fields. Once he has paired with a female skylark they will nest somewhere in one of these fields and together they will try to raise their young.

The skylark and song thrush are found throughout rural countryside in the UK and north-west Europe but populations of these and other farmland birds have declined sharply. In recent years UK populations of skylarks have plummeted by 58 per cent while the numbers of song thrushes have fallen by around 73 per cent; populations of grey partridges have dropped by 82 per cent. Another farmland bird, the red-backed shrike, can still sometimes be seen as a passing visitor in the UK. Red-backed shrikes stop off in the UK on their migratory routes, but though the odd pair might try to nest, they are now so rare that the red-backed shrike is effectively extinct here as a nesting bird.

The drops in numbers are thought to be because of changes in farmland management during the last fifty years. Herbicides reduce plant diversity and this, together with the use of insecticides, has caused severe reductions in the insect species on which many birds feed. Many farmers have now switched to growing autumn-sown cereals, which produce crops too dense for nesting in. With vast reductions in hedgerows, as field sizes expand, suitable shelter and nesting areas are now scarcer.

Researchers have confirmed that there are more species of bird and far more individuals around organically managed farmland. Crop rotation is used more extensively, so areas of land are left wild for some time. This, combined with a greater variety of crops, supports a much wider range and number of insects. Pesticides are not used, nor herbicides, so the natural diversity of plants and higher numbers of insects are multiplied. Field boundaries are managed sympathetically for farmland birds and other wildlife; hedges are planted and trimmed less frequently, so providing excellent foraging for bird species (149 species of insects live in hawthorn alone). Organic fertilizers, such as manure, are used to raise soil fertility and create rich pickings for insect-eating birds. Set-asides are also used, and these are ideal habitats for birds to forage and nest in.

Perhaps organic farming will become more popular in the future. For now, organically farmed areas are not common enough to have a major impact on European populations, but local bird species seem to have benefited whereas in other areas they are still in decline. Some efforts are being made to prevent the loss of farmland bird populations. Farmers on larger agricultural farms are paid by the government to have set-asides that are favourable to insects and birds and there are now restrictions on the use of pesticides. Farmers are also encouraged to use 'bird-friendly' methods of gathering their crops.

In some areas this seems to be working and populations are beginning to stabilize, so with concerted efforts to change current intensive farming, bird populations may begin to recover.

KJ

Union farmland, it is becoming increasingly popular, and consumer demand for organic produce is escalating due to concerns about pesticides in food and the safety of some meats following the crisis surrounding the cattle disease bovine spongiform encephalitis (BSE). Doubts are also increasing over the environmental sustainability of industrial farming practices. In 1996, organic farming in Western Europe expanded by 33 per cent yet, in the UK, demand for many organic products still outstrips domestic supply.

The two mainstays of organic farming are firstly to minimize the use of chemical fertilizers, and replace them with the ancient practice of alternating cereal crops with nitrogen-fixing crops of legumes such as peas and beans. Secondly, it aims to control weeds and pests in crops and diseases in livestock with good management and sound husbandry respectively, rather than with pesticides and other chemicals. Birds and animals have certainly benefited from such practices already.

Alternating cereals with legumes, and leaving fields uncultivated in some years, provides both food and cover for birds and small animals. A reduction in the use of chemical fertilizers, pesticides and herbicides also increases diversity in both flowers, which create a more beautiful landscape, and in insects, which provide valuable food for larger wildlife.

Poppies provide a welcome flash of red in a sea of organic wheat in Wiltshire, England. A bumble bee collects pollen from a poppy and moves on to feed in a set-aside field nearby, which is covered in a carpet of yellow bird's-foot trefoil and white clover. In a few years' time, thanks to the clover, the soil will be rich in nitrogen, ready for a crop of organic cereals or vegetables. Meanwhile the field is home to skylarks, butterflies, grasshoppers, insect-hunting swifts and a good population of short-tailed field voles. From a nearby copse, a kestrel surveys the scene. Like the red-footed falcon in Eastern Europe, the kestrel is faced with an abundance of riches. Hovering over the fallow field, the kestrel spots a vole. It stoops, grabs the vole and rises again gracefully to fly to his killing post in the nearby trees. A balanced, diverse array of wildlife can rapidly re-establish itself when grasslands are allowed to revert to a form close to their origins in the East.

Our actions, our policies and our demands as consumers have very real impacts for wildlife in the old and the new grasslands of Europe. There are many positive conservation measures which can be taken within the modern European context, but the future of many species is in the balance. We are a long way removed from the primeval woodlands and pristine steppes that covered this continent before our arrival, yet animals and plants have proved remarkably resilient and have adapted to the habitats that we have created. However, the limits to wildlife's adaptability are clearly being reached when diversity begins to plummet, as it has done in much modern farmland. Attempts to reverse this recent trend have shown great promise, however, and if there is a will to retain the riches we still have, and to encourage other species to return or increase, the way forward lies open to us.

RP

CHAPTER 5

MOUNTAINS & MOORS

THE MOUNTAIN RANGES OF EUROPE

*Nowhere is the beauty more
strikingly revealed than in the
mountains. For there flowers bloom
among dead wastes of rock, close to
regions of eternal ice... They grow in
a world of frost and heat, cold and
drought, avalanche and hurricane.*
VOLKMAR VARESCHI AND ERNST KRAUSE,
MOUNTAINS IN FLOWER

Freezing wind sweeps across a landscape of ice and snow. Flurries of snowflakes whip into the air and are sent spinning and dancing across the eerie snowscape. A tiny speck of red betrays a huddled bird: a ptarmigan, its eye wattle the only gem of colour in this white-washed world. It sits low, shuffling in the snow while the blizzard passes over. This, at the highest tops of the Alps, is life at its harshest, a landscape that has barely changed in the 12–13,000 years since the retreat of the last great Ice Age. However, this domain is one of surprise and shift, for on the Alpine mountainside fields of snow are replaced by carpets of colourful spring flowers with the change of seasons, and trickling rivulets can turn into torrential, booming waterfalls.

Europe's mountain ranges are the great spines of the continent. From the western Mediterranean to the Black Sea they dominate the land in sweeping arcs, and include some of the oldest and the newest mountains to be formed in the world. The jagged Alps, youthful in geological terms, are found in the west of Europe and the Apennines meander down through Italy. In the far eastern reaches a great arm curls around the Hungarian plain

Above
A world of ice and rock – these are the glaciated valleys of Stelvio in the Alps.

Opposite
The high, rugged landscape of the Tatra, Poland.

Inset
A lammergeier, a rare sight, soars across the high ranges of Stelvio National Park in Italy.

Above

Spring brings a burst of colour to the Alps in the shape of the Alpine rose.

plankton on the harsh winds. The organic material that collects on the icy slopes also supports some of the tiniest mountain animals: springtails. Huge numbers of these minuscule, wingless insects feed on the accumulated debris. They are extremely resistant to the cold, having even been known to revive after three years frozen in a glacier, and their numbers support a vast array of predators like mites and beetles.

VEGETATION AND WILDLIFE ON THE HIGH PEAKS

Perhaps it was on the thermals (rising currents of heated air) from below that, when the climate began to warm and the great ice sheets began to retreat, one of the first colonizers of the newly revealed terrain arrived. This was encrusting lichen, which turned ice-shattered rocks pale with lime greens, or cloaked them in warm golds and rusts. Lichens, one of the toughest but slowest growing life-forms – their cells are an intricate composite of green algae and fungus – are effective agents in the initial formation of rudimentary soil. They retain moisture beneath their crusty surface, but the water becomes slightly acidic because of the carbon dioxide released by the lichen. This slowly erodes the rock on which the lichen grows and the resulting minute particles, along with organic debris brought on the wind and broken down by animals such as springtails, all form the basis of a simple soil. This process paved the way for plants to colonize the cold, rock deserts. Hardy ground-hugging vegetation reached into the summits, while coarse grasses and berry-laden bushes advanced up the slopes until, through time, a complex jungle-in-miniature of highly evolved and specialized mountain plants, such as the dwarf willow and mountain saxifrage, formed.

This environment enabled larger insects and other animals to venture into the high territories, but they faced a tough fight for survival in the extreme climates and conditions. On the high slopes of the mountains the atmosphere is thin and dry with strong winds so, while the amount of radiation from the sun's rays is stronger, the air does not hold heat well. Wildlife here must contend with a cold, arid, tempestuous climate, high solar radiation, and air low in oxygen and carbon dioxide. As a result, a range of unique and highly adapted species have evolved for life in the sometimes arctic conditions.

Below the highest frozen ice-capped peaks, the mountainsides are still visited by seasonal snows. The winter is long and inhospitable in the Alps, but after eight months the snows begin to melt. Like a bright echo of the first spring they saw, the peaks reawaken miraculously. The ground erupts in an explosion of colour with golden snow buttercups and purple columbine, among other flowers. The delicate high mountain flora make the most of the short growing season, coating the hills in triumphant technicolor. This amazing use of colour is just one adaptation to living at such high altitudes. The vivid flowers compete for what little insect life there is, and so have a better chance of pollination.

As well as the wildlife that has specialized in survival on the high peaks, the inaccessible mountains have become a haven for some plants and animals which were once also found on the lowlands. Because the impact of human progression has been slower to take effect in the mountains those species able to cope with the climate have been able to survive in a world rapidly changing at the hand of man. Nevertheless, humans have made their mark on these peaks with grazing pastures replacing large forests. Though the creation of new habitats allowed some lowland creatures to extend higher into the slopes, survival has been precarious for other animals. This has been especially the case for large mountain mammals. However, it is due to one such creature that some of the most beautiful Alpine country can still be found intact.

The Italian national park, Gran Paradiso (derived from *Granta Parei* or 'Great Wall'), is named after a huge mountain within the park's boundaries which rises to an ice-capped peak

Below

The Retezat Mountains. Chiselled by glaciers and the passage of time, these mountains are part of the southern Carpathians and are found in the heart of Romania.

of 4,061m (13,324ft). The park, which sits on the Italian–French border, owes its existence to one of its most famous animals, the scimitar-horned ibex. Throughout Europe it had been hunted virtually to extinction, except in the kingdom of Charles Felix of Savoy. Here, too, numbers of this 'king of the peaks' had dropped to an all-time low, until in 1821 a ground-breaking royal decree was issued, which prohibited the hunting of the remaining few ibex. Victor Emmanuel II, Charles Felix's successor, impressed by the decree that had enabled the ibex to survive, continued the tradition and set up an extensive hunting reserve in the mountains. In 1921, his grandson donated the 60,000ha (150,000 acres) to the Italian state and the park was created. The remnants of the population of these ancient mountain mammals grew, and today some 3,500 thousand ibex roam the park, which remains rich with the wildlife of the Italian Alps.

On a cool summer morning you can wander up the mountain from the valley below through woods of larch and towards the higher Alpine meadows, where a wealth of wildlife is revealed. If you are patient, and sit quietly in the lush, sloping meadows among flowers such as violet Alpine asters, gentians and wild raspberry, you might get the treat of seeing one of the most lovable of the mountainside characters: the Alpine marmot. These rather chubby, large-toothed rodents can be seen munching the green grasses and any roots they can dig up. With a rolling gait they trundle up and down the slopes between patches of fresh grass and their deep, cool burrows where they must retreat when the sun is too hot for them (see box, p. 104: 'Marmots').

If you travel higher up into the peaks, another silhouette might break the jagged horizon, this one smaller than an ibex but with curiously hooked horns. Standing alert, its ears flicker in the direction of any approaching sound. In a flash it will disappear over some sheer edge or up a tremendously steep cliff-side. This is a chamois, perhaps the prince of the peaks. Renowned for its agility, the chamois' legs and hooves seem ridiculously delicate for the rough terrain that it darts over, but this belies some unusual adaptations which makes it a master of mountain travel (see box, p. 116: 'Chamois').

PREDATORS IN GRAN PARADISO AND THE CARPATHIANS

Overhead, soaring on warm updraughts, a black, shiny raven scans the jagged terrain below. Though the cloven-hoofed chamois are generally sure-footed, casualties still provide enough food for scavengers, such as ravens, to make the clifftops their home. Sharing the skies with golden eagles and tumbling flocks of Alpine chough, they clean the bones of fallen chamois and dead ibex, but these are sparse pickings. A long time ago on the cliff-sides of Gran Paradiso, the carcasses were plentiful for the opportunistic birds, provided by predators such as the wolf and bear. Although there are tiny remnant populations of wolves and bears in the mountains of Italy and Spain, the extent of the range of these great predators over the Alps is now minuscule and there are few leftovers available for the scavengers (see box, p. 30: 'Italian Bears').

Despite the precautions that the Italian royalty took to preserve their prized game animals, attitudes to predator species were somewhat different. The subject of merciless persecutions, the wolf and bear were already extinct locally by the time the hunting restrictions on the ibex were in place in 1821. The last lynx was trapped in 1914, and the last lammergeier shot in 1912. As well as the terrible loss of unique mountain populations we now know that predators are a vital factor in maintaining the ecological balance of Gran Paradiso by keeping the herds on the move and preying on weak and sick animals. Today, rather than moving steadily across the mountains in search of fresh grazing, pushed by the wolf packs that followed in their wake, animals idle for too long in smaller areas. They are also enclosed by the movements of humans across the peaks and, as a result, meadows become severely overgrazed. Furthermore, herds become isolated rather than intermingling with other herds, increasing the risk of inbreeding.

The trend in persecution of predator species was common across Europe. What drove this campaign? Were the seeds of fear planted deep in the subconscious when humans hunted the vast prehistoric forests, keeping wolves from their camps while telling tales around a fire? Or did they originate when humans first began felling trees to grow simple crops, and keep precious livestock? These were probably both factors. The people of the Middle Ages also depended on their livestock for food, and must have feared and hated predators such as the wolf. Legends of werewolves fuelled the imagination, and mountain areas, with their dark forests and wild animals, were often seen as frightening places.

There are few areas where Europe's large predators still remain in significant numbers. Paradoxically, it is in the heart of the legendary Dracula's ancient lands, a place very much steeped in superstition and still cloaked deep in forbidding forests, where bear and boar still wander and the howl of wolves can be heard. The Transylvanian Alps curl southwards into the heart of Romania at the far eastern end of the Carpathian mountain range. Towering up in a monumental stone massif, these peaks – some over 2,000m (6,562ft) high – were created around the same time as the French and Italian Alps, between 10 and 65 million years ago. The Carpathians do not reach the same altitudes as some of the western mountain ranges and so the forests grow right across the summits. Like them, however, the Carpathian Alps have been chiselled by glacier activity and worn down by time and weather.

Below the peaks, in tiny villages, life is a curious mix of the traditional and the modern. The villagers still observe the ancient customs of Romania and have a strong belief in many old tales. There is a story to explain everything, even the curious shape of the mountain from which the Retezat National Park, in the southern Carpathians, takes its name. The legend tells of how the mountain's peak was lopped off by one of the many mountain giants when, in a fit of rage, he heaved a ploughshare in its direction. The Romanian translation of the word *retezat* is 'chopped off' and, looking at its flat-topped shape, it is not hard to imagine how the story came about.

There are no giants, although chamois roam here. Hardy dwarf and Swiss stone pines hug the Alpine landscape, and encircle glacial lakes where rainbow trout snap at insects on the water's dark surface. As on the Alps, when the snow melts the spring brings a startling flush of colour to the slopes. Carpets of purple crocus burst across the landscape, framing the forbidding forests that truly dominate these lands.

Vast beech and spruce forests cloak the Retezat mountain range. They are some of the last great tracts of forested land. The industrial revolution in Romania never really took place until after the Second World War and, being land-locked, there was no need for vast supplies of shipbuilding materials. While throughout the rest of Europe the forests were felled for timber and charcoal, the Romanian mountains kept their dark woods. Invoking legend and folklore, they were maintained for a long time because of the fear that they commanded. The deeply forested and mountainous region of the Carpathians acted as an imposing border between Christian Europe and the East, and were a considerable deterrent for possible invasions by the Turks.

Even now, access into the deep woodlands is poor, and these forests are the wildest in Europe. Here the branches drip with pale lichens and moss, and the air smells of the damp, earthy soil. Narrow animal tracks are the only paths that wind among the lush green ferns and

Marmots

The Alpine marmot, with its wispy beard, snub nose and waddling gait, is one of the most endearing of the rodent family. Marmots live on the sloping Alpine meadows, above the conifer forests. Here, sitting upright among the meadow flowers, they chew their way through an abundance of roots and grass shoots. Holding the juicy morsels between their paws and turning them with their articulated fingers, they chomp their way through as many flowers and roots as they can manage, building up thick layers of insulating fat. This fat, combined with dense, sandy-coloured fur, makes it hard for the marmot to lose heat. In the hot summer midday hours they therefore have to find shelter from the sun. They retreat into the cool of their burrows where, being social animals related to the woodchuck of North America, they live in groups. Each group comprises one dominant male, his harem of females and their young.

Feeding in groups, the marmots keep a close eye on the skies above for golden eagles and ravens, two of their main predators. At the slightest sign of danger a marmot will sit bolt upright, squealing a piercing alarm call. Any marmots in the vicinity instantly make a run for cover, diving into the safety of their burrows.

The burrow systems running beneath the lush meadows can be very deep and extensive. Sometimes as much as 3m (10ft) down, they are a labyrinth of tunnels with separate chambers for latrines, nurseries and the sleeping quarters, which are lined with a thick, cosy litter of dry grass. As many as twenty marmots may live in one den system; though many of the females could breed, it appears that success may be determined by how dominant a female is. Only the highest ranking females have young, although the larger the harem is the less reproductive success she may have.

The burrows are designed to let as little wind as possible into the den, so conserving heat during the night. Entrances are made facing away from predominant winds, and are conspicuous with little mounds of earth or vegetation beside them. The steep gradient of the passage down into the nest chamber is also crucial in reducing the amount of wind that blows down the tunnels.

It is of great benefit to the marmots to live in burrows in large groups, especially when it comes to surviving the long harsh winters that come to the mountain slopes. When the temperatures fall, and the threat of snow draws near, the marmots retreat inside and block up the entrance to their burrows in preparation for a cold, eight-month hibernation. Their body temperatures and heart rates plummet during their torpor as the temperatures inside the den drop.

The marmot spends up to 60 per cent of its life in hibernation; it is a crucial and dangerous time, and some do not survive the winter. The energy they need to survive comes from the layers of subcutaneous fat built up over the summer. The marmots were hunted by humans for these fatty layers, which were used in cosmetics and thought to have potent medicinal properties. Such large numbers were taken that the Alpine marmot became endangered and locally extinct in many areas. More recently, they have been the subject of some successful reintroduction programmes across the Pyrenees, Carpathians, Black Forest and the eastern parts of the Alps.

The marmots, in their comatose state, huddle together in nests over the winter months. By snuggling close together they are able to reduce the amount of heat lost. Animals in larger harems lose less weight over winter than those in smaller harems where the young are also more likely to die. The young are more susceptible to the cold and are kept warm by the body heat of the adults, which burn off their stores of fat. Acting as a hot-water bottle for the young marmots expends a fair amount of energy, and researchers have discovered that only closely related adults will choose the energy-expensive babies as bedfellows, so ensuring the survival of their relations.

AA/KJ

Opposite

The European grey wolf. Across Europe, mountain ranges have become some of the last retreats of this now rare carnivore.

the ideal conditions of both humidity and temperature for the production of some delicious cheeses. In the Picos de Europa, the king of cheeses is *queso picón*. Made from the combined milk curds of the sheep, cows and goats raised in the area, the prize-winning smooth blue cheeses are wrapped in young oak leaves and cured in the limestone caves high in the mountains. They will ferment there for up to a year, turned frequently to make the distribution of mould even, before being parcelled up in ferns for transportation to the valleys below.

It was not until 5,000 years ago that humans began to clear the forests of the Picos de Europa for grazing, but since those first agricultural settlements there has been little change

Above

A young bear explores its world in Romania, stronghold of the European brown bear.

in the management of the land. On cliff-sides so steep that it is hard to maintain balance – quite apart from allowing access to machinery – men can still be seen with hand scythes gathering hay. Often they will tie themselves by long ropes to trees or rocky outcrops to prevent an undignified bruising from tumbling down the hill. The area and community depend on, and are shaped by, the hay meadows and pastures and the cattle that graze on them. Larger meadows are often shared by many farmers, with boundaries marked only by sticks and stones. Haymaking is then shared among the owners. Each farm tends its own herds, however. The cattle that graze the pastures are traditional breeds, such as the *casina*, which are adapted to life on the steep slopes.

Brought down to farms below the peaks for milking, the thirsty cattle are led to stream-fed troughs. Urns of milk are plunged into the cool waters where a world in miniature has become established below the surface. Taking advantage of the calm reservoir of water, Alpine newts laid their eggs in late spring and curled weed fronds around them for protection. Now the young newts gorge on mosquito larvae and on flies, attracted by drinking cattle, which become caught in the water's surface. At high altitudes tadpoles of the Alpine newt can sometimes show a retarded rate of development, called neoteny. Thought to be caused by the cold, this means that the tadpoles remain in their gill-breathing, immature stage for much longer than usual – perhaps for life – and are even able to reproduce.

Mountains
& Moors

The tadpoles of these and other amphibians, like the midwife toad, found in such man-made ponds are not alone. Dragonfly larvae lurk at the muddy bottom of this water. With ferocious speed, the lethal, extensible mouthparts of these deadly predators lash out towards unwary tadpoles which, if caught, make a nutritious meal. At the end of summer, or early next spring, the tiny carnivores will leave the trough and fly out across the valleys below on newly dried wings.

A rich wealth of insect life is found across the Cantabrian meadows. A myriad of insect visitors buzzes around the beautiful and intricate flowers. The butterflies that flit across these grasslands represent well over one third of Europe's total count, and many are found nowhere else. Here, among the lizard and tongue orchids, white asphodel and columbine, butterflies

Above

The Picos de Europa – a land of great contrasts, where lush meadows cling to the vast limestone mountains.

Opposite
*Skiers dot the
magnificent
landscape, home to
only the most hardy
of animals and plants.*

Inset
*Alpine choughs have
become accustomed to
people in the peaks.*

Chamois

Chamois are extremely well adapted to a life in the mountains. Their dainty hooves hold the key to their sure-footedness on the cliff-sides and steep slopes. When a chamois is attempting one of its near-vertical ascents up a mountainside its hooves are pressed hard against the rock surface. A dew claw, the tiny, bony extension behind the hoof which is connected to it by skin, combines with the hoof and skin to act almost like a suction cup. The daintiness of the hooves means that the chamois' weight is carried on a tiny surface area, and therefore a great amount of pressure is on the hoof as it is placed on the rock surface. The grip made under such pressure is incredibly strong and so the chamois very rarely slips. Breaking the 'cup' by a quick toe wriggle releases the grip and the chamois scampers on.

Though chamois are very wary, it is sometimes possible to see them on the higher slopes, grazing on the grasses and meadow herbs. During the summer they often migrate up to the snow-line, digging for lichens and grasses with their hooves under the icy blanket of snow. It is thought that the snow keeps them cool and deters the hordes of troublesome mosquitoes which can plague the lower slopes. The females move with their single kids in huge herds led by an older matriarch. The kids are nimble and sure-footed almost from birth and can be seen jumping on and off their mothers' backs as they practise for the precipices they will face later. Herds of up to a hundred chamois are common but, with the first heavy snowfall, the chamois split up and if possible move to woodland feeding grounds. Here they feed on what sparse scattered food they can find: buds, lichens and patches of grass that they will dig to uncover. Many do not survive their first winter if it is a harsh one because food may be scarce and avalanches take their toll.

Males are solitary roamers, but in late autumn and the early winter months, the cooling air resounds with their deep rolling bleats, as they come together with the females for the rut. The bucks chase each other, hair erect and spiky along their backs (these bristle-like hairs are coveted for the trophy hatband of a successful hunter). Potentially lethal fights are common. Chamois use a vast repertoire of vocal and visual threat displays, but in a fight they show no inhibitions about goring rivals. It was once thought that the hooked shape of their horns acted as a shock absorber if the chamois fell from the steep clifftops on to their heads, but they are actually lethal weapons in the annual rut. Stabbing towards the throat, chest and abdomen, they deliver the blows by hooking upwards. Serious damage can be caused unless the loser is quick to lie down on its belly with its neck stretched out. This passive act calms the attacker, whose aggression is soothed by the posture – which is similar to that taken by young chamois while they suckle.

KJ

CHAPTER 6

SEA & COAST

THE SEA OVER TIME

The earth is sometimes described as a 'water planet' because about three-quarters of its surface is covered by sea water. Europe's peninsula looks out over some of the richest seas in the world; there is the vast Atlantic Ocean on the western side, bordered by miles of extensive coastline, while the Mediterranean Sea stretches below, separating Europe from Africa.

The oceans and lands have not always patterned our globe with the present familiar shapes. Though apparently solid, the earth's crust in fact acts like a very viscous liquid, moving in slow but vast currents and dragging with it the great areas of land that make up the continents. As the land masses move, clashing together and being torn asunder, new mountains, coastlines and ocean floors are formed. The Atlantic Ocean was originally created by a huge 'supercontinent' of land that separated into what we know as Europe, Africa and the Americas, leaving a gap that was filled as primeval oceans flooded into it. The seabed beneath the North Sea was once a great desert plain, created as the land masses drifted, and was not flooded until 100 million years ago at a time of great changes in the sea level.

The sea levels are dependent on how much water is locked up in the great ice-caps of the North and South, which has changed over time. The level of the sea at the height of the last

Above

The waves of the Atlantic Ocean pound the west coasts of Europe, helping to shape the shoreline.

Opposite

The seven-armed starfish, a voracious predator among the rock pools on the south-west coast of Ireland.

Inset

Urchins using discarded shells, perhaps as a kind of 'sun-hat', to protect them from the sun's rays in the shallow, exposed rock pools.

The huge stretch of the Atlantic separates the Americas from the European and African continents. Its rich waters have supported some of the oldest and best-developed fishing industries in the world, especially for cod and herring, while coastal waters provide rich and varied harvests. On the most southerly part of the Iberian Peninsula on Europe's Atlantic coast is Santa Luzia, a small town of no more than 2,000 people. Nestling in the south-east corner of Portugal, close to Spain, this little coastal community perches on the banks of the Ria Formosa, a coastal lagoon. In the outskirts of the town, storks' nests sit precariously on chimney-stacks, and on the marsh rafts of flamingos shimmer delicately pink in the salty heat of the midday sun. The Ria Formosa has its own microclimate; it is an important sanctuary for marine wildlife, and is protected and preserved as one of Portugal's national parks. Santa Luzia itself looks iridescent, for it is bathed in brilliant sparkling light – as only found in places close to the sea. Its dazzling whitewashed houses seem to vibrate in the sunshine. Colourful painted tiles decorate the walls and give a clue as to what supports this little town. They depict a sea creature that inspired legends of monsters of the deep, but which in reality is as interesting an animal as the behemoths of the wildest tales could be.

Santa Luzia depends for its living on the skill of its fishermen for hunting not fish but octopuses. It is over the last fifty years that fishing for octopuses has developed here, but the local fishermen use a technique that was depicted in mosaics by the ancient Romans over 2,000 years ago. Their daily routine is dictated not only by clocks but also by the tides; when the sea allows enough water in, their brightly coloured wooden fishing-boats can leave the lagoon and make for the open sea. A pastel-pink dawn lights the way for the fleet, scattered offshore, as they gather their strange harvest. The fishermen use clay vases, just like those used on land for storage, to capture the octopuses. Strung together, about 3m (10ft) apart, the pots are lowered to rest on the sea floor. To an octopus these pots seem to offer a safe retreat from the open and exposed sandy seabed, where shelter is at a premium.

Once the fishermen reach the buoys that mark the location of the pots below, their good-humoured camaraderie subsides and a quiet air of determination takes over. With the aid of a winch they lift and check the pots, evicting any resident octopuses on to the deck. If the weather is fine, an eight-hour shift can see over a thousand pots lifted before the fleet returns home. This method of fishing has no harmful side-effects on other marine life, for unlike drift-net fishing, which captures everything in its path, it is specific to the octopus. It also has surprisingly little effect on octopus populations. In order to win such a prime location an octopus often faces stiff competition from other octopuses, so the successful occupant is usually a good size and mature, and not an undersized juvenile. Also, if the pots get lost at sea they are immediately colonized and become harmless tiny reefs for a host of marine creatures, in contrast to lost and entangling nets that pose a threat to man and beast alike.

At low tide, among the grounded fleet of fishing-boats, fiddler crabs emerge from their holes in the mud and feed on the exposed emerald algae that grows there. The mud-flats may not look as spectacular as towering cliffs or golden beaches, but the fiddler crabs and other occupants of estuarine mud-flats are residents of one of the world's richest habitats. When mud accumulates in coastal lagoons or estuaries it is often mixed with quantities of rich organic material, made up of decaying plants and animals brought in the tides or washed down by rivers. This material is then deposited where the currents slow down. The surface of the mud may be green with vast mats of algae, but it is the thousands of tiny snails found below the surface that make the mud-flats so attractive to large flocks of wading birds and, when submerged, to shoals of fish. Also hidden in the sand and mud are cockle-beds, providing a harvest for humans; this both supplements the local community's diet and forms the basis of a trade that has existed for thousands of years. These ancient ties with the sea still provide a livelihood which is regulated, and so sustained by nature itself, for only when the tide is extremely low can the cockle-pickers gain access to these rich beds.

Humans have exploited all shoreline habitats from the low-tide shores to the high Atlantic-facing cliffs. Portuguese cliff fishermen still practise the time-honoured art of fishing from dramatic cliffs 100m (330ft) high. This practice, in addition to considerable fishing skills, also requires a good head for heights. These are the most westerly shores of Europe and you can look out, from the heights of the magnificent cliffs, at the Atlantic Ocean stretching into the distance. The vast Iberian currents sweep past these shores before they meet with the most northerly 'arm' of the great North Atlantic Drift (see box, p. 123: 'Currents'). Where the surface water is moved away from the land, by the flow of the currents, cold water from the depths wells up to replace it. This deep Atlantic water is rich with nutrients from decaying organic matter that has long since sunk to the bottom. Such areas of upwelling water occur infrequently – in just 0.1 per cent of all the world's ocean area, but they account for about 25 per cent of the world's annual fish catch. The deep Atlantic still remains a rich source of seafood, but in the last few decades Europeans have overfished even this great stretch of ocean on an unprecedented scale. As a result, the great tuna and sardine fisheries have sadly declined.

Above

A common dolphin, one of the many dolphins and whales found in the waters around the Azores.

The rich Atlantic waters off the islands of the Azores, 1,500km (900 miles) west of Portugal, have always been home to a wide variety of whales and dolphins. Among the most gregarious are the pilot whales. These dark torpedo-shaped cetaceans (a term which places them in the dolphin/whale family) are actually a type of dolphin, despite their name, 'pilot whales'. And like dolphins they travel in big groups ranging in size from anything between ten and several hundred. When travelling in pod formation they may swim abreast in a line several kilometres across. The mother–calf bond is extremely strong and the female may suckle the calf up to two years of age. As they surface, the very young calves can be seen throwing their heads clear of the water in order to breathe, whereas adults usually only show the top half of their heads. The adults may dive for up to ten minutes or more, and feed on small fish and squid.

Here, too, schools of common dolphins speed through the waters. They may have travelled together from the Straits of Gibraltar, splitting into smaller groups and then re-forming during the course of the day. Dolphins are extremely social animals, living in groups of anything up to a hundred or more. Less common are interactions between dolphins and whales. However, sometimes baleen whales, such as fin whales or Sei whales, have been spotted travelling through the waters with groups of dolphins. Perhaps the whales are attracted to dolphin activity by associating them with the vast shoals of fish that dolphins will follow through these waters, and on which they both prey .

wide-mouthed, rubber-lipped fish – have evolved to merge into the background, their patchy red and brown coloration serving them well as camouflage. The pelvic fins of all blennies, including the tompot blenny with its distinctive bushy 'eyebrows', are reduced to finger-like projections. They use these fins to prop themselves up in a characteristic pose as they keep an eye out for prey, intruders to their territory, and any predators that might attack from both above and below the surface of the water.

Many rock-pool inhabitants are extremely opportunistic. As well as scavenging on the rock-pool floor, they will try to eat any animal smaller than themselves or vulnerable to attack. Even limpets, apparently secure in their hard, cone-shaped shells, and glued to rocks with an iron grip by one huge, muscular foot, have their predators. They lift up their shells while grazing the fields of algae across the rocks and, if extremely quick, a crab might manage to flip over the limpet, so exposing the fleshy foot. Normally, however, limpets clamp down with amazing speed and strength to the rock surface, making them impossible to move.

One predator that is found in rock pools specializes in feeding on shellfish, such as limpets and mussels. Carried along by thousands of tiny tube-like feet, the common starfish advances across the rock-pool floor towards a limpet. If it gets a strong enough grip, it can, with the combined strength of its suckered feet, pull the limpet off the rock surface. However, the limpet has evolved an extraordinary counter-attack against the starfish's advances. The limpet chemically senses the approaching starfish and immediately raises its shell high off the ground. Looking like a dancing mushroom, it sways back and forth, preventing the starfish from getting a secure grip either on the shell or the rock base. The limpet then begins what is known as 'stomping'. Holding its shell far away from the rock it then begins clamping down, quickly and repeatedly. If a starfish arm gets in the way it will be trapped between the sharp shell edge and the hard stone, perhaps causing serious injury. This is a life-and-death struggle, for if the starfish is not deterred, then the limpet will be swamped and eaten alive, and if the starfish becomes trapped it may itself be exposed to other predators for a while.

One of the main predators of the common starfish is the seven-armed starfish. It is a larger, fiery-orange creature, the tiger of the starfish family. It has longer tube feet, which end in tiny pointed knobs instead of suckers, and moves much faster than the common starfish. It therefore soon catches up with its retreating prey and positions itself on top. The seven arms quickly place themselves over those of the smaller starfish and the long tube feet reach down on either side, tenting the common starfish's arms and locking them together in a tight embrace. In this position, the seven-armed starfish can evert its stomach over the centre of the smaller starfish, and it rapidly begins to digest its body. The common starfish can lose one of its arms to the larger predator, which will draw its white, sack-like stomach containing the limb up into its body cavity. If one arm is enough to fill the stomach of the seven-armed starfish then it might relax enough, while digesting its bulky feast, to allow the common starfish to make a slow getaway on its remaining four arms. Astonishingly, the common starfish is very likely to survive and continue its precarious existence in the pool despite having lost nearly a fifth of its body. Starfish can regenerate lost limbs, and slowly a stumpy arm will begin to replace that taken by the large predator.

The presence of tube feet, or 'podia', are one indication that the starfish is a distant relative of the sea urchin. Spined and nearly spherical, these animals are familiar to many people as the empty, pretty-coloured shells, or tests, which can be found on the beach – or, more likely, in the beachside souvenir shops. The urchin also moves on tube feet, but these are much longer and thinner, and deep purple in colour. In many rock pools along the south-west coast of Ireland, purple urchins completely dominate the pool floor. Thousands upon thousands of them cover rocky shelves and cram together on ledges and platforms wherever the conditions allow. They browse on seaweed and algae, using the sharp teeth of an amazing mouth structure called the Aristotle's lantern. This is found at the centre of the urchin's base and comprises five hard, sharp-pointed plates or teeth, each shaped a little like an arrowhead and arranged in a tight circle. With these 'teeth' they scrape at the algae-coated rocks and can pull and tear at pieces of kelp. Although some of these urchins move freely around the pools at night, other urchins typically bore deep into the rock for protection from wave action and, by creating their own miniature water pools, avoid desiccation at low tide. Boring into the rock with their spines and the teeth of the Aristotle's lanterns, some of the urchins are believed never to leave the cavity. They feed on the algae that forms on the inside of their cavity and drag pieces of kelp down under their spiny shells towards their teeth.

En masse, urchins on the rock-pool floor look like an enormous mattress of thorny spines, which is enough to deter most predators. However, these prickly creatures also feel the need for further protection which they form from old limpet and mussel shells, and pieces of kelp which they place across their exposed crowns. If the rush of the incoming tide has knocked off the coating of shells, then the urchins will quickly begin to draw surrounding shells nearer with their far-reaching, suckered tube feet. Grasping the shell, they pass it from foot to foot over their near-spherical bodies until the shells sit atop them like tiny plates of armour. Sometimes there are even tiny anemones on the shells, which make the urchins appear decorated with colourful, living bonnets. It is thought that the shells are either for camouflage and additional protection against predators or protection from the ultraviolet light in the sun's rays when the tide is out, as the urchin's outer layer of skin (which is above the calcareous layer) is very delicate.

There are thousands of molluscs living in the rock pools: periwinkles feed on the seaweed, mussels filter the seawater, while limpets graze the algae from the rocks. When they die or are preyed upon, their soft bodies are nibbled away to leave only the hard shells, which accumulate in their thousands in rock pools and across the sea floor. Many marine animals take advantage of this constant supply of ready-made armour, some moving inside while others pull them on top.

Scuttling across the rock-pool floors are the hermit crabs, which have specialized in living in the abandoned shells of whelks and other molluscs of the rock pools and sea floor. They are extremely aggressive towards one another and, if they do collide, the meeting involves much claw-waving and the eventual retreat of the smaller crab. They are scavengers, feeding on dead shellfish or other animals, and any other titbits they can find. However, in order to grow, the crabs must find a larger shell of the right size and weight into which they can move. In a rock pool where there is a healthy population of hermit crabs, these may be in short supply. The selection process is often fraught with difficulty and danger as, after carefully taking a measure of a new shell with its nimble claws, the hermit crab must then try it out for size. Quickly jumping out of the old shell, the crab pushes its soft and vulnerable body into the new shell and retreats inside. The tiny crustacean seems to shuffle around a little but, hopefully, the new mobile home is the right fit, and light enough for the crab to move. If for some reason it does not pass the selection test, then the crab must rapidly jump back into its old shell and begin the search anew. The desired shell need not be always empty. If it cannot find a suitable empty shell then the hermit crab may resort to a take-over bid, evicting another hermit crab from its home.

Among the rubble of pebbles and shells another common animal of the deeper rock pools stirs. It is one of the spider crabs, superbly camouflaged by a mound of shells and vegetation.

This spider crab takes the art of camouflage and decoration to extremes, and lives not inside one shell but under a great mound of them, or anything else it can lift from its surroundings to make itself disappear into the background. Part of its outer shell is covered in small Velcro-like hooks that fasten shells and algae on to the crab's back as surely as if they were glue. The green and coralline algae found on its back may even have taken hold and be growing there – the crab itself becoming a kind of mobile home. Gathering periwinkle and limpet shells from the sandy bottom with its nimble, chopstick pincers, the crab places each article carefully on

its back with fine and precise movements. With a final jump and shuffle it kicks the surrounding sand and shells into the air and they drift back down through the water to settle over the crab's camouflaged back. Now, only two tiny, red, beady eyes poke out of the shell pile to betray the creature beneath.

THE UNDERWATER WORLD

As land-based creatures humans have for a long time looked upon the ocean's surface, observing the constantly changing colour and 'moods' of its waters. We have swum in waves as children, fished its depths and explored even the most remote coastlines but it was not until recently that we could freely move beneath the waves. With the discovery and development of deep-sea exploration submarines and, later, scuba-diving, a new world of discovery was opened up to us. However, the world's oceans have long fascinated scholars and scientists. Studies of the sea and oceans, and the life below the waters, have been dated to earlier than

Above

Under attack!
A limpet defends itself
against predation by a
common starfish by
'mushrooming up'.

Opposite

The rhythm of the
tides shapes the lives
of all animals and
plants on the
shoreline.

the fourth century BC when Aristotle studied the waters of the Aegean and commented on the ideas of previous philosophers. Oceanography, as it was later called, developed in leaps and bounds during the nineteenth century, and it was not until then that we began truly to understand the enormous and complex processes that maintain the underwater world.

The very basis of this hidden life comes from the mass of microscopic organisms that float in the 'soup' of ocean water. At the mercy of the currents and actions of the sea, this collection of tiny plants and animals, some as big and complex as they will ever get, others in the larval stage of much larger organisms (such as lobsters and crabs), is known as plankton (from the Greek *planktos*, which means 'to wander'). With very few exceptions, all life is linked by the flow of energy that originates from the sun. Plants harness the energy of sunlight and here the web of life begins. Using that energy, they convert carbon dioxide and mineral nutrients into the proteins, sugars and starches with which they grow and on which animals live. In the sea, nine-tenths of this plant life is found in the plankton, drifting mostly in the upper 30m (99ft) layer that is penetrated by sunlight. At least three-fifths of plankton is made up of single-celled plants called diatoms. Several million may be present in a litre of water; they are thought of as the sea's pasture as they provide grazing for thousands of animals, from two-spot gobies to blue whales.

Copepods, the world's most numerous multicellular animal, are found in the planktonic soup. They are red-brown crustaceans which, although no bigger than a pinhead, can devour 130,000 diatoms a day. The herring, a fast-swimming, slender fish, feeds mainly on the copepods and can have as many as 7,000 in its stomach. This would mean that the herring could be digesting up to 1 million diatoms every few hours.

One of the great events of the sea year, although we do not see it, is a spring explosion of the plant – and therefore animal – life in the waters around the European coasts. In the dark midwinter months, plankton levels are low. In March or April, the sunlight returns and the sea temperature rises slightly, triggering reproduction of life on a massive scale. Diatom populations bloom; one diatom may, in one month, give rise to 1,000 million others, and soon the waters are filled with tiny plants. Taking advantage of this huge increase of easily available food, hundreds of species of fish, crustaceans and other marine life spawn and reproduce at this time as well. The sea waters teem with countless numbers of young invertebrate larvae and fish fry, which feast on the minute plants.

Remarkably, minuscule plankton sustain one of the largest of all creatures in the European coastal seas, the basking shark. This enormous creature can grow to around the size of a double-decker bus, but remains an enigma to us, as very little is known about its lifestyle or movements. However, what we do know is that in the summer months, when there are sometimes successive plankton blooms, the basking shark can be seen near the water's surface, trawling the sea with its mouth agape. Hoovering up the plankton, this briny monster can filter over 1,000 tonnes of water an hour with its gill plates. The copepods, diatoms and other tiny organisms stick on the shark's gill plates and the shark then swallows them down. At the end of the summer feast the basking shark disappears once more, probably into the deep waters off the continental shelf. This, the largest fish in the North Atlantic and second-largest shark in the world (growing to weigh more than two elephants), is entirely fed and nourished by some of the smallest organisms in the sea.

Among the floating nomads of the oceans are jellyfish. As they steadily pulse through the water they can – to some extent – power their movement and direction but are largely at the mercy of the currents. Goose barnacles, too, might be considered a larger type of plankton because they attach themselves, at the very early stages of their lives, to floating objects. These large barnacles hang from rubbery stalks below the surface and extend their fan-like cirri, whirling them around in the water to catch much tinier plankton. Often found in bits of flotsam and jetsam washed up on the shore, it was once thought – perhaps because of their long, neck-like stalks and similar colouring – that barnacle geese emerged from the shells of these arthropods. Ancient manuscripts portrayed the migratory geese hatching from the stalked shells. This phenomenon was considered an explanation for their sudden appearance at their spring feeding grounds. (It has been suggested, however, that the legend was invented by hungry Christians, giving them the excuse to call the goose a fish and so allowing them to eat it on Fridays and during Lent.)

COASTAL BIRDS AND SEALS

Plankton are an important food source for fish which, in turn, support vast populations of coastal birds. Guillemots, often called the penguins of the northern hemisphere because of their waddling gate and their ability to apparently fly under water, are actually members of the auk family. They are superbly adapted to life not only on the sea's surface but also underneath it. Chasing little fish such as sand eels, they slice through the water; their wings are specially designed for amazingly agile underwater manoeuvres. Most of their fishing is done within 20m (66ft) of the water's surface, although they are known to be able to dive as deep as 60m (198ft).

Guillemots spend most of their lives at sea but they have to come on to dry land in order to breed and raise their young. This they do *en masse*, congregating on inaccessible high cliffs on the mainland and remote offshore islands. Over 10,000 guillemots converge on the Farne Islands off the north-east coast of England where they nest, safe from ground-based predators that cannot make the couple-of-miles crossing from the mainland.

Most of the mating pairs breed at the same time, with two-thirds of all eggs being laid within a ten-day period. Every space is taken on the rocky outcrops, which become swamped by the black and white birds. Nesting all at once, and in such close proximity, has its advantages. With so many anxious parental eyes scanning the horizon, airborne predators, such as black-backed gulls, are often spotted before they can make an attack. The guillemot chick is fed for about three weeks on a rich diet of sand eels, and both parents take an active part in the feeding duties. As with many bird species, pairs that breed successfully tend to bond for life.

A parent returning with a fresh catch for the chicks has no trouble in homing in on the nest location. However, once it has found the approximate site of its nest it must make sure that it feeds the right chick, for there are plenty to choose from. Incredibly, while still inside the egg, the chick began to call with its own unique sound, which the parents learned. As it returns from fishing the parent listens for this familiar call and so ensures that it is feeding its own young.

Guillemots are not alone in seeking the sanctuary of these islands. Puffins nest here as well. These plump little birds, like the guillemot, spend most of their life out at sea, coming ashore only to raise their young. Around 15,000 pairs nest on the Farne Islands, an even greater number than the guillemots. However, the puffins lay their eggs deep in burrows dug into the soft, grassy slopes of the islands, and so their numbers are less apparent. Parents are seen only on their 'delivery round' when they fly ashore with furiously beating wings to land outside the burrow entrance, their brightly coloured bills laden with silver sand eels.

Unlike the ungainly airborne puffins, gannets, the largest seabird in the North Atlantic, seem to command the skies. They are the ace divers of the seabird world, attacking their prey from on high. The large cream and white birds converge in the skies in their thousands above the waters rich with shoals of fish. One by one they fold their wings to plummet at nearly ninety degrees to the water, and at a speed of 80km/h (48mph) before plunging through the surface. Rocketing down through the panic-stricken shoal, they snatch fish in their beaks and then rise back to the surface with their catches. They re-emerge to a surface that bubbles with the splashes of other gannets as they, too, make their dive. Such a quick-fire aerial bombardment helps to confuse shoals of fish, so increasing the chance of a catch.

From a distance it seems there is a blizzard above Bass Rock, an island just a few kilometres north-east of the Farnes. The gannets spin in dizzying circles over the rocky

Above

A puffin in its full breeding regalia returns with a good catch of sand eels.

lump of the island, and the seas surrounding it, and the air resounds with the clamour of their calls. Below, the surface of Bass Rock shimmers with the white plumage of 70,000 nesting gannets. Their nests fill every available space and are often in very regular rows, with each nest positioned just out of reach of its neighbour's beak. With so many gannets in the roost it pays to recognize your mate and reaffirm the pair bond. A breeding pair of gannets will groom each other each time one returns from a fishing trip, and will go through complex greeting rituals, gently wiping each other's plated bills and calling out in excitement.

These great northern bird colonies are testimony to the riches of Europe's seas, which draw birds from around the world to nest on these shores. Terns migrate from their wintering grounds off the African coast to breed on some of the more remote shorelines and islands of Europe. Some of these terns land year after year, joining the puffins and guillemots, to nest on the Farne Islands. A miniature kingdom of birds, the Farnes have long been an important refuge for wildlife, thanks largely to a seventh-century saint, who sought solace on these quiet islands. Perhaps because of its seemingly gentle and very tame nature, the eider duck had a special place in St Cuthbert's affections. He established laws, the first of their kind in Britain,

to protect them during their breeding season. However, St Cuthbert valued all forms of life. Under his protection, and from that time onwards, the islands have been a haven for all of the plants and animals found there.

Four species of tern nest on the Farnes including the common, the Sandwich, and in small numbers of perhaps around twenty, the beautiful roseate tern. The Arctic tern, of which there are around 3,000 to 4,000 pairs, nests in the largest numbers on the islands. Island wardens learned quickly that these birds have a very different temperament to the eider ducks. The terns protect their chicks, which huddle in a simple ground nest, from anyone foolish enough

Above

The Farne Islands have been a sanctuary for common terns since the time of St Cuthbert who lived on the islands in the seventh century.

CHAPTER 7

LAND OF ICE & SNOW

THE ARCTIC REGION IN EUROPE

...the vast sweep of the Arctic Zone, and those forlorn regions of dreary space – that reservoir of frost and snow, where firm fields of ice surround the pole and concentre the multiplied rigours of extreme cold.

CHARLOTTE BRONTË, *JANE EYRE*

It is midnight at Norway's North Cape in the northernmost part of mainland Europe, and a full moon glows brightly in the sky. Strangely, it is lighter now than it will be in twelve hours' time at midday. In winter, between October and April, this is a land of the night and mystery. Here, near the top of the world, is a place of permanent darkness in winter and permanent light in summer.

Every now and then bright flashes of green, white and sometimes red or pink flicker in the never-ending black sky. Silent curtains of coloured light ripple among the stars. This phenomenon is the extraordinary aurora borealis, the northern lights. The effect is caused by charged particles from the sun striking gases of the earth's upper atmosphere and illuminating them like neon lights. They tend to be most spectacular at times when sunspot activity and solar flares are at their peak.

About 320km (200 miles) before you run out of road, as you drive north in Norway from Trondheim to Narvik, you meet an ice-covered road sign that reads 'Arctic Circle – 66° 32′ North'. The Arctic Circle, which is the southern border of Arctic Europe, is not just a line of latitude on the map; it has an

Above

Glacier ice drifts into the ocean.

Opposite

The dramatic icy landscape of Europe's most northerly land, Svalbard.

Inset

A little auk on guard outside its nest burrow.

North Pole

G R E E N L A N D

Limit of permanent pack ice

GREENLAND SEA

SVALBARD

Effect of Gulf
Stream

Maximum limit of drift ice

BARENTS SEA

Arctic Circle

NORWEGIAN SEA

N O R W A Y

During spring the hours of daylight lengthen at the Arctic Circle and the landscape starts to change. The sun brings warmth, and with that comes life. The vast rivers that drain the central highlands down to the rugged west coast and to the north have been frozen solid during the long winter months. The sun now starts to release the energy from within the rivers. As each day grows longer the ice, with massive creaks and explosions, breaks into huge blocks, some the size of cars. They are swept away at terrifying speed, crashing and tumbling toward the ocean.

The Norwegian coast is a jagged, rugged place. Steep cliffs rise up from the icy ocean and fiords. The sea-filled, deep valleys reach inland, many for several miles. Offshore it is equally rugged: hundreds of islands form a protective barrier from the North Atlantic Ocean. Tiny fishing villages crouch on any available land, for these seas provide some of the richest fishing in the world. The huge numbers of fish attract sea eagles, otters and orcas, the killer whales.

As the sun melts the last of the snow on the narrow coastal plains, white turns to fresh new green. In a perfect display of natural timing, hundreds of barnacle geese glide in from their winter feeding grounds in the Solway Firth in Scotland. Although they have flown 2,000km (1,200 miles), this idyllic place is merely a temporary resting-place – a refuelling stop on their journey to their summer breeding grounds in the high Arctic. Watered by the melting snow and warmed by the sun, the grass grows quickly. Within a week the rested and fed geese are ready to make their next incredible journey north. This time it will involve crossing the Barrents Sea and navigating to the tiny nesting area that they will have used in previous years on a group of islands only 1,000km (600 miles) from the North Pole. Timing is critical. If they arrive too early snow will still cover the grass and they may be frozen or starved to death. If they arrive too late the best nest sites will be gone, the breeding season will be short and their chicks may not survive the summer.

As the geese head north they cross an ocean that changes from rich blue-green to speckled white, and then to pure white – an ocean that, in the north, is frozen. The islands in the group known collectively as Svalbard rise dramatically out of the Arctic Ocean to a height of 1,700m (5,610ft). Made up of four main islands, surrounded by hundreds of small ones, their total area is about the same as that of Belgium and the Netherlands together. With a population of only 3,000, concentrated into four settlements on the warmer west coast, this is truly an empty place.

Svalbard, 600km (360 miles) due north of Norway, is the largest group of islands above the Arctic Circle and has almost sixty glaciers. These are permanently moving walls of ice. Svalbard was previously named Spitsbergen and is still called this on many maps, but this name now correctly refers only to the largest island. Svalbard means 'Cold Coast' in Norwegian, and is technically a no man's land; it does not belong to any one country although it is managed by Norway. Svalbard guards the Arctic Ocean and the Barents Sea to the north of Russia. More importantly, Svalbard is also another kind of natural boundary because it marks the southernmost limits of movement of the permanent sea ice. In winter the sea is totally frozen from the south of Svalbard all the way to the North Pole. In summer the edge of the ice retreats to the top of the islands.

Because of the cold, Svalbard, like most of the Arctic region, is also very dry; there is hardly any snow or rain. The freezing air precipitates the little moisture in the air as frost so that even in winter, although the landscape is white, it snows very little – perhaps 0.5m (1½ft) at the most. An incredible 60 per cent of Svalbard is covered in permanent, year-round ice. Glaciers are common and, where they reach the ocean, huge and impressive ice walls silently wait until the pressure of millions of tonnes of ice pushing from behind forces blocks to

wind and currents will smash the ice together, breaking it into a slurry. Huge icebergs will be washed up on to the beaches.

THE ARCTIC SUMMER

By early July, with temperatures of around 5°C (41°F), it is true summer in the high Arctic, although there is still snow and ice in shaded areas where the reindeer can go to keep cool in their well-insulated coats. The cliffs that tower to over 300m (990ft) above the narrow coastal plain echo with the constant, noisy clamour of nesting sea birds in what seems like an organized apartment block. In the rocky scree at the base, pairs of little auks are sharing the brooding of their eggs in their deep, rocky burrows. The noise from the attending mates is deafening as half a million birds make this one of the largest nesting colonies in the world. There is a constant toing and froing as birds fly backwards and forwards to the fishing grounds – little auks have to put much effort into flying because of their short, stumpy wings. The most noise created, however, is when the colony is disturbed by either a fox or a patrolling glaucous gull, one of the birds of prey of the high Arctic in the absence of true raptors. If a fox or a gull is seen by an auk the whole colony will take off with a tremendous vocal noise and huge wing-fluttering. Wave after wave of birds launch out over the sea and fly round and round, in what must be one of the bird-world's greatest natural spectacles. When the threat goes the auks gradually settle in a wing-flapping flurry, returning to the rock at the entrance to their nest tunnel. But the vocal clamour never ceases, day or night.

The lower ledges on the vertical cliffs above the little auks are mostly inhabited by Brunnich's guillemots, another species of the auk family, sometimes known as the 'penguins of

The Polar Bear

It has been suggested that polar bears are among the newest species of mammals on earth, and that they developed from an isolated Arctic coastal population of brown bears possibly as recently as the last Ice Age. Polar bears are recognized as the largest of all terrestrial carnivores. Males are more than twice the size of females – the average male weighs 500kg (1,100lb), whereas the average female weighs 200kg (440lb). The polar bear is, on average, longer, taller and heavier than the largest brown bears, which are its closest relatives. Polar bears are white except for the tip of their nose, their claws and the dark flesh of their gums and tongue. Physically, they differ from brown bears in that they have longer necks, smaller heads and somewhat sharper teeth, making them better adapted to a meat diet.

Polar bear behaviour is centred around their way of life, which consists mainly of hunting seals. They spend most of their lives on the sea ice because that is where the seals are. They are adapted to this habitat in many ways. They are protected from the cold by their warm fur and thick layer of blubber – sometimes protected too well as they become overheated if they exert themselves for a long time, which explains their usually unhurried demeanour. Their huge paws, with furred soles, serve as snowshoes when they walk and as paddles when they swim. Their cryptic coloration is not a protection against predators; polar bears had none before human hunters arrived. Instead, it helps to conceal them as they pursue their usual prey: seals, especially ringed seals.

The most common hunting method used by polar bears is 'still-hunting'. First, a polar bear uses its acute sense of smell to find a seal's breathing hole; then it sits in wait until the seal comes up for air, whereupon it pounces. Sometimes a breathing hole will be roofed over by a snow crust so strong that the bear must use all its strength to break through it. Less frequently, polar bears stalk their prey. They do this in warm weather, when seals often haul themselves out on to the ice to sun themselves.

Polar bears eat a variety of other foods. Sometimes they catch swimming sea birds by swimming under them and attacking from below. They have been known to kill belugas (white whales) trapped in small pools by moving pack ice; very occasionally they capture young walruses. But polar bears are not exclusively carnivorous: they dive for kelp, and when the sea ice is nearly melted in late summer, forcing the bears on to the land, they enjoy berries. When food is scarce, a bear conserves energy by going to sleep, often in a hollow it has dug in the snow to shelter itself from the wind. If necessary, polar bears can even slow down their metabolism to tide themselves over a period of food shortage.

AA/NA

jumping continues, the gulls have eaten so many that they no longer kill the chicks. Nevertheless, they still wait for them, and even move in as though they are going to attack. However, instead of attacking they just stand and watch as the chicks run by on their short, webbed feet, constantly falling over because of the penguin-like upright stance that makes them too top-heavy for high-speed running.

But it is not certain death for a chick that does not manage to glide right out to the ocean. Some will make the long stumbling walk across the grass through the rocks, tumble and roll down the bank to the beach and cross the sand to the waves without harm while all the predators are busy with other hatchlings. On busy nights, hundreds of chicks are making their flight to the water and although food for the foxes and gulls is literally falling out of the sky there can,

Above, left to right

1. An Arctic fox in its thick white winter coat.

2. Svalbard's towering sea-bird colonies.

3. Purple saxifrage blooms among the rocks.

4. Brunnich's guillemots defend their cliff ledges.

sometimes, just be too many. On occasion, if a chick crash-lands short of the ocean, an adult will land as well and push and coax the clumsy fledgling towards the water. This can be successful – the adult can chase off a hungry glaucous gull – but it can be a risk for the parent birds, as a fox can attack and kill it as the chick escapes. Because of the risk the adult rarely lands to help the chick but usually flies on to the sea where it calls continually to guide its offspring.

The fox cubs will often hunt chicks with their mother to learn the technique but, as the summer progresses, they become more proficient and will chase the guillemot chicks on their own. However, an inexperienced fox cub can sometimes have a surprise: the chick will fight back, running at the fox and sometimes – if the fox is unsure and slightly timid – the chick can get to the water unharmed. Very occasionally a glaucous gull will actually snatch a gliding chick in the air. This is rare and involves precise flying from the gull because it has to dive down from above, more like a bird of prey.

Although many Brunnich's guillemot chicks are killed on their maiden flight to the ocean, most do successfully join the rafts of thousands of birds. Along with the adults, they will move offshore to the rich fishing grounds in order to grow their flight feathers fully and follow the ice edge for the winter until they return to the high cliffs the following year.

Another bird that rests on the foreshore beneath the cliffs where all this drama is taking place is the Arctic skua, a dramatic-looking and superbly acrobatic flier which makes its living by stealing food from other birds and chasing them until they give it up. Skuas will defend their offspring with more aggression and energy than almost any other bird. When a possible predator starts to get close one of the skuas will fly down from their usual vantage point, the highest boulder in their territory, and start behaving strangely to draw the predator away from their chick and towards themselves. Normally, they will start by stretching out a wing and staggering around, looking injured. This, of course, might work with a fox, which would see the skua as prey, but it does not work with the reindeer whose only interest is in the thick, lush grass that it is trying to eat as quickly as possible to build up its strength for the mating season in the coming autumn.

Autumn comes
birds feed thei...
weather starts. ...
is over, the gras...
wind has starte...
nesting birds a...
and the Arctic f...
still twenty-fou...
and clouds cove...

The guille...
islands. These...
perch for thes...
because most p...
their parents, ...
they lose all th...
caught by foxe...
their incredibl...

Soon the s...
the polar bears...
will be totally ...
and October, ...
than the islan...
mountains, lak...
moose and the...
species of the ...
the river flood...
remove the vel...
each year. Unti...
is at this time t...
will chase off o...

In autumn...
and many berri...
bears they are ...
lack of suitable...
ice-bear cousin...
whole year rou...
by lowering the...
nourishment. ...
bears as this is t...

In Sarek, a...
approaches. To...
remove the las...
As in the high ...
wilderness are...
light returns, b...

Once the skua sees that the reindeer has not been drawn away, it will start to rip up moss and grass aggressively and throw it around. This strange behaviour has no effect on a grazing reindeer and therefore the skua must use its full weaponry. For a full-blown serious attack both skuas perform an aerial bombardment, each bird swooping down at high speed, narrowly missing their target. Usually this will quickly have the desired effect and a pair of skuas can often start a mini-stampede of eight to ten reindeer fleeing back to the overgrazed areas around the skuas' territory. To really make their point the skuas will sometimes even pull hair from the reindeers' backs. Foxes, obviously, are a much greater threat than reindeer to the skuas, their eggs and their chicks. Skuas will see them off with even more effort, although in their attack they have to be more careful, as the fox will fight back by jumping and snapping at the diving birds.

PEOPLE IN THE ARCTIC

Although the Arctic, as already mentioned, is the largest true wilderness area in Europe, small numbers of people have in fact lived here for a long time. It is, however, an incredibly hard place in which to exist as most of it is plunged into semi- or total darkness during the winter,

CHAPTER 8

CITIZENS

OPPORTUNITIES FOR WILDLIFE IN CITIES

Europe's cities and towns are growing at a phenomenal rate. A land area equivalent to the size of two football fields is covered by urban development every minute. Two per cent of European farmland is swallowed up by the urban spread every ten years. Only forests are increasing at a faster rate than the city jungles, and these two growth areas are inextricably linked. More and more people have abandoned traditional ways of living in the countryside and moved into cities over the millennia, and that trend is still continuing over much of Europe. As managed countryside is abandoned, natural forests are beginning to reclaim much land that was once grazed, particularly in central and eastern Europe, and many forests of fast-growing conifers are being planted, particularly in north-western Europe. More than two-thirds of Europe's human population now live an urban life, and the proportion keeps rising.

As the towers of concrete and glass go up and vast areas of tarmac are laid, what is the impact on the wildlife of Europe? Can animals and plants find homes in the new cityscapes, or are they retreating as fast as the countryside is? Loss of natural and traditionally managed landscape is undoubtedly bad news for many forms of wildlife, and a continent covered in tarmac would be a sterile place indeed. But for some forms of wildlife, cities

Above
Kittiwakes nesting on window ledges above a busy market street in Newcastle, England.

Opposite
White storks cruise past the Spanish city of Segovia, heading for the local rubbish dump.

Inset
An urban fox emerges at dusk in a London cemetery.

are becoming an increasingly attractive draw: despite their noise, dirt and the hustle and bustle, Europe's cities support a wealth of animals and plants, some of them obvious and numerous, many of them hidden and surprising. The great variety of city wildlife reflects its diverse origins; some creatures have lived with humans ever since the first settlements arose, some have spread alongside human civilization, and some have only found a way to live with us in the last few decades. A number entered cities by choice, others found themselves trapped as woods were enclosed. Some discovered habitats such as city rivers, canals, lakes and parks, which met their needs in the same way as country waterways and woodlands did. Others found the city warmer and safer than the wilds beyond the city boundaries. Some exotic species arrived as stowaways in produce brought through trade from afar, and a number found themselves released after losing favour as pets. Whatever the origin, the way that wildlife has coped in cities is the ultimate example of nature adapting to human changes to the landscape, and is one of the greatest success stories in Europe.

Remarkably, the diversity of plants and animals in cities is often higher than in the surrounding land, especially where the advance of modern farming techniques has led to a more uniform landscape of vast, chemically sprayed fields growing the same crops. Cities, by contrast, can provide an incredible mixture of openings for species capable of, or allowed to, take advantage. The infiltration of wildlife on to our streets and into our parks and gardens has had a chequered history, though; the city is a challenging place for nature, since animals have often been viewed as pests and many plants as weeds. The success of city wildlife today reflects both changes in our attitudes to wildlife and the incredible opportunism and adaptability of plants and animals. So when and where did the story begin?

EARLY CITIES

The invasion of cities by wildlife goes back to the time when the world's first permanent settlements were built, around 10,000 years ago. The establishment of villages, towns and cities, which accompanied the spread of ordered, communal living or 'civilization', was based firmly on the advance of agriculture. Before the first cereals were domesticated from wild grasses, and the first grazing animals domesticated from wild oxen, sheep and goats, most groups of human hunter–gatherers would have been forced to lead fairly nomadic lives. They followed the migrations of wild animals and the waves of growth and fruiting by various plants from lowlands to highlands and from south to north as the seasons changed. Even those peoples who could live in one area for the whole year could only have lived in very low densities; a maximum of around one human per square kilometre (0.4 sq mile) has been estimated. The guaranteed, year-round food that domestic herds and crops provided allowed the same area of land to support around fifty to a hundred times more people, and settled, dense communities, supported by the surrounding land, arose for the first time.

Although settled communities are based on agriculture, one definition of a city describes a sizeable community of people, most of whom do not grow food but live on the surplus created by others and contribute to society in other ways. Cities became centres for commerce, administration and culture. These advances first occurred, as discussed in Chapter 1, in the Middle East. The oldest settlement known, at Jericho, dates from 10,000 years ago. From that time on, civilization spread rapidly, largely in a westerly direction, towards and into Europe. The people who lived in the world's first large town, Catal Huyuk, left few clues as to their relationship with wildlife beyond their obvious worship of the wild bull or aurochs, and we do not yet know whether any creatures regularly lived alongside the people in this early city.

Since the first agriculturists reached Europe, however, the cities they built have left us with a few more clues as to how city wildlife established itself.

The first European cities were built on Crete, midway between the mainland of Greece and the coast of North Africa. Permanent settlers are thought to have come to the island around 8,000 years ago from the mainland of what is now Turkey, bringing domestic animals and cereals with them. Their first known settlement was built at Knossos, which was set in a fertile valley in the north of the island, around 6000 BC. Excavations at Knossos show that a settlement was maintained here throughout the Neolithic period until 2600 BC. The buildings of that era had ground floors of stone and upper floors built of mud and branches. The population of Knossos, and of Crete generally, rose rapidly over the next few centuries, around the time that bronze tools began to be used. As farming became more efficient and trading with other islands and people around the Mediterranean began, the Minoan civilization, Europe's first great culture, developed and flowered from about 2600 BC until 1100 BC. The remains of dozens of towns, palaces and country villas survive from this era, and their excavation has revealed a great deal about Minoan life.

The remains of the Minoan town of Gournia and the multi-storeyed palaces built within the settlements at Phaistos, Knossos and Malia are perhaps the most intact and impressive today, and give a hint of how things might have looked in Minoan times. These settlements were tiny compared to many modern European cities, but they were the focus of rural populations whose numbers may not have differed much from today's. It has been estimated from the extent of settlements discovered and on estimates for how many people agricultural land can support, that about seventy to eighty people inhabited each square kilometre (0.4 sq mile) of farmed land in Minoan times. By estimating that a third of Crete would have been cultivatable then, the total human population may have been around 200,000 to 250,000 in Minoan times, as opposed to about 500,000 now.

The largest Minoan settlements never spanned more than a few hundred metres, and may never have housed more than a few thousand people. They were surrounded by a rugged landscape comprising a mix of cultivated plains and hillsides terraced for growing vines and olives, along with largely untamed mountain slopes and woods grazed by goats. Plants and animals from the surrounding limestone countryside must have strayed into the cities and the rampant anemones, poppies and other wild flowers growing among the ruins today have no doubt always seeded themselves wherever there was the slightest opportunity. For many plants there is little difference between sprouting between the merest cracks in natural limestone boulders on the hillsides, and taking their chances in crevices between the blocks of marble and the limestone that paved the Minoan squares and streets. They may even have suffered less from the attentions of the goats which, to this day, graze the hillsides of Crete. Balkan green lizards and ocellated skinks bask on the lichen-encrusted stone walls and artefacts today, and no doubt did the same thing 4,000 years ago while the Minoans went about their daily lives.

The Minoans had very organized plumbing arrangements: extensive drainage systems sloped downhill towards major central sewers, up to 2m (6½ft) deep, and at Knossos water was carried 10km (6 miles) along clay pipes from Mount Juktas to supply the palace. But however organized they were, it is very likely that flies were encouraged by a concentrated presence of humans, and would have provided an extra lure for lizards. It is impossible to know how the Minoans reacted to plants and animals infiltrating their cities, but it is quite likely that they welcomed their presence; much of their art was inspired by nature, and accurate portrayals of many creatures and plants appear on their vases, jewellery and burial casks.

long ago, some recently. Their success varies greatly depending on what different cities provide and on the attitude of the human residents to wildlife.

Today, kestrels perch on the spires and rooftops of the magnificent twelfth-century cathedral of Notre Dame in Paris. These raptors kill far more mammals and birds than lesser kestrels do, and their conversion to city-living is relatively recent. Their presence in cities has only been recorded in the last hundred years or so, but they have done well ever since. Five pairs of kestrels nest in the walls and roof of Notre Dame alone, and a further fifteen or so pairs nest in Paris, using such notable addresses as the Arc de Triomphe, the Eiffel Tower, and the smartest high-rise office blocks of the modern financial centre, La Défense. In London, kestrels first nested in 1930, but now there are over a hundred pairs. A similar story of urban penetration by kestrels has been repeated across the other great cities of Europe.

Urban kestrels have been carefully studied, and a remarkable story of adaptation in the way they hunt has emerged. Tall buildings with ledges and gaps in stonework and under roofs provide excellent breeding sites and high vantage points, much as natural rocky crags do. But for those living in the heart of a big city, commuting to the countryside to hunt – as the lesser kestrels of Trujillo do – takes too much time and effort. The Paris kestrels hunt exclusively within the city, which provides for all their needs. The city kestrels' cousins in the countryside feed mainly on insects and small mammals, hunting largely by hovering before dropping on to their prey. In cities, however, populations of small mammals are lower, and urban kestrels have successfully switched to alternative prey, including many birds.

In Paris, sparrows are perhaps the most plentiful target the kestrels can spy on from the heights of the cathedral. Sparrows have long been numerous in cities around Europe, and have become hugely dependent on humans for food. Some believe they would all but die out if it were not for our presence. They once benefited greatly from feeding on undigested seeds in the plentiful horse manure that was around in the days before motor vehicles. Today they survive on seeds, leftovers and hand-outs, for which they are never too shy to beg. They nest in roofs, streetlamps and even ornate carvings all over Paris and other big cities. Sparrows may have come

Below

A white stork arrives at its nest in the medieval heart of Trujillo, set in the dehesa *landscape of Spain's Extremadura region.*

Rats are by far the most widespread and numerous wild mammals in European cities, and have become the supreme urban specialists, often outnumbering human residents. There are actually two species of rat in Europe, the black and the brown rat, both of them immigrants from Asia.

The black rat, which originated in South-East Asia and parts of China, reached Europe first, spreading westwards through India to the Middle East via the trade routes. They have always been closely associated with human settlements, and bones in a Roman well in York show they were present in Britain by the fifth century AD. By the Middle Ages they were well established throughout Europe and carried the fleas responsible for the outbreaks of bubonic plague, or Black Death, which ravaged Europe in the fourteenth century. Black rats are true city specialists and almost invariably live around buildings, warehouses, supermarkets, food-processing plants and ships. They are largely nocturnal and eat almost anything, including vegetables. They live in groups that defend their territory from outsiders, and breed at an alarming rate when conditions are good for them. Black rats are still found throughout most of Europe, but today they are vastly outnumbered in Britain and Scandinavia by the brown rat, which copes better with the cold.

The brown rat, *Rattus norvegicus*, arrived in Europe in the early part of the eighteenth century, probably on cargo ships travelling from the East. It has smaller, hairier ears, a shorter, thicker tail and smaller eyes than the black rat. Its stronghold is also the city, but it can cope in the countryside as well, especially in summer. Brown rats are less strictly nocturnal than black rats. They are more carnivorous, and their social life is one of their great strengths. Large colonies can develop rapidly from the offspring of a single pregnant female.

The history of rats as carriers of disease is impossible to deny. Since the arrival of antibiotics and the link between rat fleas and disease became known, the threat of plague has receded. Rats, however, still carry about seventeen diseases that can affect humans, many of them potentially fatal.

Rats are virtually impossible to exterminate once established, as trapping only controls their numbers and always leaves a surviving population. Poisoning is also rarely very effective, as rats are exceptionally wary of unfamiliar foods, and learn to avoid poisons quickly. If a rat does become ill from poisoning, other rats know from the smell of its breath what food to avoid. If a rat eats a new food, however, and remains healthy, the others are also encouraged to try this new food. Even if a population is reduced by trapping or poisoning, the surviving rats' rate of reproduction increases to compensate. These endlessly adaptable and highly intelligent creatures are true survivors.

AA/NU

floods in the sewer, and a rapid rise in water level can flood some nests out. A mother will quickly react to any such danger, and in a matter of minutes scamper back and forth to a higher nest site, carrying each baby by the scruff of the neck in her teeth. She will bound across the sewer at its narrowest point and rescue them before the old nest is flooded out. A mother rat will even go back to collect the bedding if she has time in order to settle her brood in as comfortably as possible in their new home. Then she suckles them all and gives them a thorough clean, licking them carefully as she turns them over in her paws. As the flood subsides, she will go out to feed and will usually find all sorts of new foods washed down by the flood.

Such scenes show that there is definitely a more endearing side to the rat's nature, and domestic rats make friendly, intelligent pets. Because of the diseases wild rats spread, however, most cities wage a constant war against them. Poisoned bait is regularly placed at intervals along city sewers. Nevertheless, such poisoning tends to control rather than reduce populations as rats are so good at learning to avoid the bait (see box, p. 169: 'Urban Rats').

CITY WATERWAYS

Where storm drains flow out into city rivers, the rats may also forage on the banks of the river alongside a wide variety of other wildlife. Rivers and canals provide one of the best refuges in the city for countryside species. Many plants and animals adapted to freshwater living find everything they need in city waters as long as it is not too polluted. Fish rapidly die if the water becomes too stagnant and short of oxygen, but where the water keeps flowing, and only treated sewage is allowed to flow into city waterways, a diverse invertebrate and fish fauna can build up. This encourages ducks, moorhens, and even the occasional dipper and kingfisher to live in city backwaters.

Recently a small mammal, which is often mistaken for the rat, has increasingly ventured into city rivers: the water-vole. This animal, sometimes called a water-rat, is even more aquatic than the rat, swimming and diving strongly by paddling all four feet. The water-voles have much softer, rounder faces than rats, and live largely by grazing green plants on the river banks and by scavenging on the occasional fish. These animals were strictly country dwellers until recently but in many parts of Europe, especially Britain, country populations have been devastated by mink, escapees from fur farms, and so water-voles have disappeared from much of their former range. They have always had predators in the countryside, but none that can follow them into the water and down their burrows as the mink can. Water-voles are increasingly finding refuge in cities, even major conurbations such as Birmingham, where a number of thriving populations now live. It seems that the mink have been unable to follow them here, since they need a wider diet of rabbits and other creatures to survive on, which they cannot find in the city. So, as long as the river is not too polluted, and there are earth banks where they can make their burrows and vegetation to feed on, water-voles seem set to continue their quiet invasion of our cities. Few people are aware of their presence, which is true of much city wildlife.

NIGHT CREATURES

As daylight fades, another small mammal whose presence often goes unnoticed in cities begins to awaken near the river-bank. Daubenton's bats are often found nestled into crevices or hanging from the roofs of storm drains and under bridges in central and northern Europe. These little bats are nearly always associated with water and, as night falls and they take wing,

Returning home late at night in the city of Brasov in Romania can be an alarming experience, especially if there is a rubbish skip close to your home. Brasov is surrounded by dense mountain forests which support one of the highest populations of brown bears in Europe. These huge animals have learned that there are easy pickings on offer in the city, in the form of tasty titbits among the municipal rubbish. As the evening light fades, the bears make their way along regular routes from the forests to the food-laden skips that line the streets on the edge of town.

The noisy activities of the bears in the skips do not go unnoticed by the local dogs, but a single dog barking at them is soon seen off. Sometimes the local dogs band together to try and drive the bears back into the forest. If the bear has a full stomach it may amble off with the dogs barking at its heels, but this is a dangerous pursuit for the dogs. One swipe from a bear's paw would kill a dog instantly.

The bears, especially protective mothers with cubs, are also potentially very dangerous to people, and the locals have learned to give them the respect they deserve. Bears are usually shy around people, but the Brasov bears have become increasingly bold. Some of the skips are positioned in front of a block of flats, and residents returning late at night often encounter the bears. Passing cars, however, are largely ignored and cars that slow down are usually just given a hard stare. Some bears will leave if a car stops and people get out, but many just stay and watch warily, even as people walk past the skip on the other side of the road. At least two Romanian householders have reputedly been savaged when they have surprised bears going through their dustbins, and some measures have been taken to try and deter them. A few of the skips are now protected by bear-proof concrete bunkers and occasionally the bears have been shot at with salt pellets, though this tactic rarely keeps them away for long. It is more likely to send them to a different skip further down the street. Scientists are also now beginning to study the bears, and at least one family has been radio-collared, so that their movements both in and around the city can be monitored.

Traditionally, close exposure of bears to humans usually leads to disaster, since attacks from provoked bears are likely to lead to retaliation and increased pressure to kill them. Hopefully, by understanding the movements and needs of these bears better, a way to protect the wild population can be found alongside deterring them from using the city as a hunting-ground.

NU/JC

they start to hawk up and down low over the river. They hunt by echo-location for small aquatic flies and other insects dancing above the water. Like all European bats, they are completely harmless, since they are strictly insectivorous. They are at risk themselves from rats, which have been known to attack and kill them in their roosts if they can reach them.

Unfairly, bats have been the subject of a great deal of fear throughout Europe, perhaps because of their largely silent, little-known ways and their outlandish, wrinkled faces. The strange leaf-like shapes of many bat noses help them to focus their high-pitched echo-locating squeaks, and their large ears pick up the echoes bouncing off walls and prey. Other kinds of bat often use roof spaces and cracks in house walls to roost and breed in, and sometimes enter the living spaces of houses, although usually these are merely young bats which have made a mistake. Such encounters have spawned many dark folk-tales around Europe. Bats in houses were once thought to be the devil seeking out someone in the house to take them off to hell. In Finland, it was once believed that the souls of humans took wing in the form of bats while people slept. In reality, urban bats do nothing but good, ridding cities of many biting flies and other insects.

The bright lights of cities have proven to be a great bonus for bats and some other city creatures because lights attract many insects to dance in confused circles around them. A large number of insects, including moths, migrate at night using the light of the moon to navigate. Bright artificial lights are thought to muddle such insects, which mistake them for the moon. Moths can navigate in straight lines by flying at a fixed angle to the distant moon. If they mistake a bright city light for the moon, however, they have to change direction as they approach the light to keep the angle the same, and end up spiralling in towards it. Many city bats have learned that streetlamps are happy hunting grounds and, on warm summer nights, they flit quietly around the lights and rivers of both small towns and great cities. The lovely city of Pisa in Italy is particularly rich in bats; they can be seen pouring out of the cracks in some of the ancient buildings lining the banks of the River Arno, and flitting around above the streetlights as throngs of people come and go from the many bars and restaurants of the city.

Insects drawn to the bright lights of cities attract other forms of nocturnal night-life. In Rome, as endless streams of traffic surge past the beautifully floodlit Colosseum, geckos sit quietly on walls all along the Imperial Way, where Roman soldiers once paraded in triumphal processions. They are waiting for insects, drawn by the lights to settle on the floodlit stonework, whereupon the geckos sprint with surprising speed, flick out a sticky tongue and snaffle a meal. They are very shy, and if disturbed, always have a handy bolt-hole to dive into at a moment's notice. Some have managed to get the best of both worlds, combining protection with a constant supply of insects, by living within the glass surrounds of streetlamps. The best spots are prized by these small lizards, which are highly territorial. If a strange gecko wanders into its patch, a resident gecko will rush out and bite it and, unless the intruder is much larger, will continue the attack until it is driven off. The strange nocturnal courtship calls of geckos can be a little disconcerting for some, but these little creatures are largely accepted in cities, since they do no damage and act as mobile insect traps. They have actually done very well out of city-living. Thanks to the extra food lured by the lights, the abundance of walls to hunt on and hide in, and the extra warmth they can seek out in winter when many retreat to chimneys, fireplaces and behind radiators, geckos live at higher densities in cities than outside them.

Unlike the harmless bats and geckos, another European night creature seems intent on causing problems by waging a war against car owners. An increasing number of cars in Switzerland and Germany have had their electrical cables attacked during the night. For some time the cause of this nocturnal damage was a complete mystery, but the sharp-toothed culprit was eventually identified as the beech marten.

Urban beech martens in Switzerland are secretive animals. They have lived with humans for a long time, sharing houses, gardens and lofts. They are often heard scampering around at night, but they are very rarely seen. They are great opportunists and live on anything they can find, with our leftovers featuring large on their diet. But why do they repay us by attacking, or 'martenizing', car cables? The answer has only recently been discovered. They are highly territorial animals, and mark all sorts of objects within their territory with their scent to warn off intruders. A car parked within their domain gets this treatment as well, especially the nice cosy area with its network of electrical leads around a warm engine, which makes a snug temporary resting-place for a marten. In the countryside, major features of their territory tend to stay put, but the rules are different in cities. New cars keep appearing in their patch and have to be checked out. If it has been already scent-marked by a marten in another territory, there's trouble. The incensed resident reacts as if its territory has been invaded, and aggressively savages the offending scent-marked cables with its teeth. The mystery is solved but, short of never moving your car, no easy solution has yet been found to the problem.

THE LURE OF URBAN WASTE

In eastern Europe, animals capable of damaging far more than a few cables are drawn into some of Romania's cities. Brasov is surrounded by steep, forest-covered hills, and some of the forest's dwellers make their way into town at night to take advantage of a universal city product: rubbish. Cats and dogs scavenging in the large municipal rubbish skips need to be on the alert because some visitors to these skips are quite capable of eating them for dinner. The rubbish skips and bins of Brasov have become favourite foraging grounds for families of brown bears. These huge creatures pad quietly out of the woods late at night, and make their way by well-worn paths to the skips to see what delights have been put out during the day. Mother bears, often accompanied by up to three playful cubs, clamber up into the skips to rummage around in search of food (see box, p. 173: 'The Bears of Brasov').

Bears are not the only large mammals to come into this city. A team of scientists has been closely monitoring a population of wolves living in the forests around Brasov. By radio-tracking some of them, backed up with infra-red filming, they have discovered that certain wolves regularly make their way into the city to scavenge on rubbish and to hunt for cats and dogs.

Urban waste has had a huge impact on all sorts of creatures over the millennia, and the increasing use of landfill sites in the last fifty years has had a major impact on the populations of some wildlife. In northern Europe gulls have been the main beneficiaries, and many landfill sites attract gulls in their thousands from first light, when fresh rubbish starts to arrive at the site. Municipal rubbish dumps in southern Europe also attract hordes of birds, but here they can be very different. The landfill site a few miles from the old city of Segovia in central Spain attracts large flocks of white storks, which pick over the rubbish. These birds not only benefit from nesting-places in the city, but also from this year-round supply of food. Not all the storks migrate south to Africa for the winter, and those that stay can supplement their diet with the rich pickings on offer at the city dumps. The storks are joined by large groups of black kites in the summer, which swoop down among the storks and a few cattle egrets, grasping at morsels of food with their talons, and scattering flocks of starlings. Griffon and Egyptian vultures also visit some southern rubbish dumps, joining the storks and kites. Dozens of them visit a dump near Tarifa in southern Spain around the time that many of these birds have just arrived on their spring migration from Africa.

Above

*A feral pigeon falls
victim to an unlikely
predator in a London
park – a white pelican.*

SQUARES, CEMETERIES AND GARDENS

The great public squares of our cities, like great clearings in a forest of buildings, have also proved a great draw for hordes of another kind of bird, the feral pigeon. Perhaps the most famous and dramatic example is St Mark's Square in Venice, where up to 4,000 pigeons jostle for space with the tourists, and beg for food from them. Venice has a total population of about 20–25,000 pigeons, and people's reaction to them is sharply divided. For some, the chance to feed them is all part of the Venice experience, and street vendors can make a living selling corn for the birds. Such behaviour by us is quite a turn around, since feral pigeons are largely descended from birds kept for food since ancient times! For others, however, the pigeons are nothing but bad news. Some 74 tonnes of pigeon guano is produced in Venice each year, and the birds often raid market places and other food stores, and can also spread diseases. Many favour wholesale extermination of them (see box, p. 180: 'Feral Pigeons').

The feral cats of Venice do their best to help this cause, and can often be seen stalking pigeons in St Mark's Square. There are nearly 5,000 cats living in colonies all over the city. People have very mixed feelings about the cats as well, but, under Italian law, they cannot be killed or even moved from where they are living, since they are traditionally viewed as useful controllers of rats and mice. Unfortunately, they take many songbirds too, and they can spread diseases. Many believe that their numbers are out of hand in Venice, aided by the many cat-loving people who feed them, and a programme of catching, sterilizing and releasing them has been implemented for several years now by the city council to control their numbers.

The pigeons in St Mark's Square are not just hunted by the cats, of which they have become extremely wary; a new danger stalks the square that many are quite unprepared for. One solitary herring-gull, a rather depressed-looking specimen with drooping wings, perhaps reflecting a past injury or disease, has become an efficient pigeon-killing machine. For the last four years or so it has wandered among the hordes of pigeons in the early morning, before making sudden dashes and snatching them from behind in its powerful beak. Without the talons of a raptor to pin its prey down, it simply holds on tight and slowly squeezes the life out of its victims before pecking at the corpses to feed. This shocking and unusual behaviour upsets pigeon-loving tourists, who often chase it off. However, dispossessed of its prey, it simply strikes again, and often kills two or three pigeons in a day. Herring-gulls are known to attack chicks of other species, and sometimes even of their own, but this rogue pigeon-killing gull seems to be a one-off. It is, however, typical of the way that city wildlife can adapt to take advantage of opportunities in the city. It may even prove to be the first of a new wave of 'killer' gulls. Introduced species have caused similar havoc elsewhere. A pelican living in a London park has also taken to snatching the odd unsuspecting pigeon, and the park wardens try to keep it well fed with fish to prevent it from exhibiting this quirky behaviour.

The quiet of city cemeteries provides a contrast to the hustle and bustle of the great squares, and they are havens for a variety of shy creatures such as squirrels and foxes. Cemeteries often date back centuries, and are frequently set on hilltops or woodlands that were once outside the city, but which have been swallowed up by urban spread. Much of the original woodland wildlife of these areas has been able to persist in these islands of green, but has had to learn to live alongside humans. In London, all sorts of people visit cemeteries to relax, to meet friends or to jog, but some come specifically to interact with the wildlife. Grey squirrels, originally from America, have now all but replaced the red squirrel in Britain. They are retiring creatures in the countryside where they are classed as vermin for the damage they do to tree bark, and are controlled by gamekeepers. But in city cemeteries they are safe; people often befriend them, calling individuals by name to feed them, sometimes from the hand.

Foxes build their earths under the bushes of some London cemeteries, and although they keep themselves largely hidden during the day, some people are aware of their presence and visit on a daily basis to put meat, bones and other scraps out for them. The foxes keep out of sight while there are people around, but start to emerge from their lairs as a police car goes round asking people to leave. As soon as the gates are shut, several emerge at once, bringing their cubs with them to hunt for the food that has been left for them. Some people have found ways to watch the foxes from the gates – throwing food in through the railings and watching the foxes creep out in the half light to collect these gifts. They go on feeding here after dark, often within a metre or so of passing cars and pedestrians who are quite unaware of the foxes' presence.

The hedgehog is another country mammal that is increasingly making a home in European cities, and for this animal the well-tended lawns of our gardens are a great attraction. Here, they can find all sorts of insects, such as beetles, and one of their favourite foods: earthworms. People are often unaware that hedgehogs are visiting their gardens, but

Above

Many people visit St James's park in London to feed a wide variety of wildfowl, both ornamental and wild.

they may well hear them without realizing what is making the noise. Hedgehogs are surprisingly noisy for small animals. When two males meet, one will sometimes charge the other and try to push him off his feet, rolling him over and over, and emitting loud grunts. But this is nothing compared to hedgehog courtship. If a male encounters a female, he begins to circle her. She turns in order to face him all the time, emitting a constant stream of gruff, grunting, hissing sounds. He continues to circle her, sometimes for hours at a time as she continues to grunt, or follows her in large circles around the lawn. Eventually she may lay down her spines and allow him to mate with her but, long before that point, the householder may come to investigate the noise, thinking that intruders or perhaps courting human couples are in the garden. Some people have even called the police in alarm. The timid hedgehogs usually scuttle off without being seen, and the mystery of the backyard grunts still baffles some city households. Hedgehogs have to some extent been driven to feed in city gardens as their countryside homes have often become less diverse and productive. With the increasing use of pesticides and herbicides, along with the removal of many hedges to create larger fields in much of Europe, hedgehogs have less to eat and fewer places to live in the country.

As cities have grown, and people have begun to demand more green space around their homes, extensive suburban fringes have developed around most European cities. Small areas of original woodland have increasingly been enclosed within sprawling regions of leafy suburbia. A shy country mammal, the badger, has often found itself living in the city by force of circumstance rather than by choice. Badgers can survive in suburbia if their setts are left undisturbed, and if they can find enough food, natural or provided for them, in gardens. Many people appreciate having these attractive creatures in their gardens and put out a range of foods for them such as nuts, honey and bread. These normally timid animals can become used to house lights and even floodlights, and allow quiet house owners to watch them feeding. They will always dig for their own food, however, turning over flower-beds and making holes in lawns in search of insects and worms. They will also attack any hedgehogs they encounter; badgers are one of the hedgehog's few natural predators. But, as they do in the country, urban hedgehogs will move out if they detect the smell of badgers. Where badgers live in the fringes of cities, as they often do in Britain and Scandinavia, hedgehogs gravitate more and more to the centre of town to avoid them. Urban badgers range quite widely over several square kilometres, visiting lots of different gardens to take any food that is put out for them or to dig for it themselves, but they always return to their home sett before dawn.

In the cold light of day, the damage badgers can cause is only too apparent: pock-marked lawns, dug up flowers, huge mounds of soil around their setts and the occasional collapsing wall or garden shed that has been undermined by their burrowing. Unsurprisingly, some residents hate badgers with a vengeance. In Britain, at least, they are protected, and if people choose to build houses in their territories, they should perhaps expect to find these animals trying to make a living around them.

Our gardens can support a surprising diversity of wildlife if we accept it. Because every garden tends to be different, with a different array of grasses, flowers, shrubs and trees, many of them imported exotic species, gardens create a wonderfully diverse habitat for animals to exploit. High plant diversity encourages high insect diversity, which in turn provides food for a variety of birds, and sometimes reptiles and amphibians as well, especially if the garden has a pond. Garden ponds are becoming an increasingly important refuge for frogs, toads, newts, dragonflies, damselflies and other freshwater species whose numbers have declined in much of north-west Europe as country regions have become less varied and more prone to the impact of pesticides. Some people even encourage insects like butterflies by planting a wide array of flowers which bloom in succession so providing much sweet nectar for them. Buddleia, a flowering shrub, originally from China, acts as a particular magnet for butterflies. In Britain, red admirals, peacocks, painted ladies, small tortoiseshells, commas, brimstones and cabbage whites sometimes all cluster on these bushes on a warm day in late summer. Nowadays it is not unusual for suburban gardens to boast a higher diversity of insects than the surrounding countryside, and it has been estimated that up to a third of Britain's insect species visit a single 0.6-hectare suburban garden in the city of Leicester in the Midlands. Gardens are also becoming increasingly important for birds and they can be amazingly rich in the variety and numbers found in them. Mature suburban gardens can support higher densities of breeding birds than the richest deciduous woodland.

Gardens are also important for birds in winter because bird tables and bird-feeders provide vital food supplies. Some suburban gardens in Britain now attract over thirty species of birds to them in winter. Some species, such as siskins, greenfinches, goldfinches and long-tailed tits, have only started visiting gardens in the last fifty years. This move to the cities and towns reflects how some habitats have been lost in the country as agriculture has become less mixed. It also reflects how more people are putting out a wider range of foods, including a very small type of seed from Africa called niger, which goldfinches in particular favour. Birds are also, quite simply, learning to take advantage. It is thought that siskins may first have come to gardens by mistaking orange string bags of peanuts for pine cones, and quickly realized their lucky mistake. This feeding behaviour, which began in the west of Britain, has spread rapidly; more and more of these tiny yellow finches are visiting gardens these days.

Blue tits learned how to peck their way through metal milk-bottle tops to get a free drink some sixty years ago in the Midlands in Britain, and this behaviour has spread across most of the country since then. Some magpies have recently discovered that cartons of eggs delivered to doorsteps are also worth attacking. In time, more species are likely to discover increased opportunities for themselves in cities, and the trend of city wildlife becoming ever more diverse and numerous is set to continue.

It is not just native species that have learned to take advantage. In many countries in Europe populations of ring-necked parakeets, originally from subtropical Africa and Asia, are establishing feral populations, which visit gardens in winter looking for food. These acrobatic birds will balance on washing lines to peck at strings of peanuts in their shells which have been pegged out for them. Small family parties will visit individual gardens, but this gives no impression of how many now live in some cities. At the end of the day, however, the families begin to gather together into flocks, and head for a safe roosting site. They always use tall trees, which can be almost anywhere, but the open spaces of sports grounds have become quite popular: one roost at a London rugby football ground now attracts around 1,000 of these exotic, noisy birds on a winter evening.

CITY CENTRES AND PARKS

These 1,000 birds, however, pale into insignificance when compared with the 2 million or so starlings that head for the centre of Rome every night in the winter, creating one of the greatest wildlife spectacles anywhere in Europe. For, as the starling flocks head for their roosts, they are hunted by peregrine falcons. In their efforts to avoid being caught, the starlings create remarkable patterns in the evening sky. Some ten peregrines now patrol the skies over Rome every winter, each taking a starling or two every night, but their impact on the starling numbers are minimal, and the vast majority makes it safely through to roost. Starlings choose the city

Feral Pigeons

The feral pigeon is one of the great urban specialists, living in cities throughout Europe. Its relationship with humans goes back a long way, but the nature of its bond with us has changed radically over the years.

Feral pigeons are descendants of rock-doves, which still breed on sea cliffs and rock-faces in many European countries. They come in a wide range of colour forms and patterns, but many still look very like the rock-dove, with a white rump and two black bars on silvery wings. Rock-doves

were probably first captured and domesticated by Neolithic people around 5,000 years ago, and there is clear evidence that pigeons were kept by the ancient Egyptians, Greeks and Romans as well as the Moors, all of whom designed ornate lodgings for the birds. They kept them for food, and colonies of pigeons became very popular. Living within the grounds of castles, monasteries and towns, the birds foraged efficiently for themselves in the surrounding countryside but returned to their 'designer' homes to breed, and so provided a constant supply of fresh meat and eggs for the owners. Over time, various races of pigeons and doves were bred, and lofts and dovecotes were built for them throughout medieval Europe. After the agricultural revolution of the early nineteenth century, the need for pigeons as food declined, and ways to rear and store other kinds of meat also developed.

It is uncertain when feral populations first became established, but it seems that many escapees headed straight for the cities, using the high ledges of buildings to nest on, much as rock-doves use cliff ledges. By the late fourteenth century, they were definitely nesting on St Paul's Cathedral in London, since the Bishop of London complained that the windows were being broken by people throwing stones at the birds. Three centuries later, as the Great Fire of London ravaged the city, Samuel Pepys wrote in his famous diary that 'the poor pigeons were loath to leave their houses, but hovered about the windows and balconies till they were, some of them, burned and fell down'.

Pigeons have continued to thrive in cities to this day, and their success stems from a huge change in their relationship with humans. Far from providing food for us as they once did, we now provide much of a modern city pigeon's diet. Great public squares, like Trafalgar Square in London, and St Mark's Square in Venice, have become havens for pigeons, to which many people come as much to feed the pigeons as to admire the architecture.

As well as finding plenty of food in our cities, pigeons have learned to exploit a wide range of nesting sites. They now use not just city ledges, but also many roof-spaces and any abandoned buildings and warehouses they can find their way into. Pigeon breeding ghettos can be very squalid places, with piles of droppings, dead birds and broken eggs building up in thick layers. At high densities, the pigeons become very defensive over their nest sites and aggressive with one another. A combination of aggression, stress and the increased levels of both parasites and disease, leads to high mortality in overcrowded colonies. Diseased birds can spread Salmonella bacteria and other diseases to humans. Their droppings also cause a lot of mess and damage, making them very unpopular with some people. Firm pigeon-control measures have had to be taken in some cities, but there is no doubt that urban pigeons are here to stay, whether we welcome them or not.

AA/NU

Starlings in Rome

As the sun sets over the city of Rome, and the sky turns red behind one of the greatest cityscapes of all, vast flocks of starlings stream in from the countryside, passing close to the great dome of St Peter's Cathedral on their way to one of the three or four massive roosts within the city. As the starlings arrive, peregrine falcons take to the wing to hunt them.

An aerial ballet of sublime beauty unfolds as a life-or-death struggle is fought out against the blood-red sky. The peregrine's aim is to swoop down on an unsuspecting bird, but the flocks are wary and bunch together tightly, trying to get above and behind the falcon. Enormous black clouds of starlings, moving as one, often track single falcons which become dwarfed by the pursuing flocks. But if the falcon can get above them and dive in among the flock, havoc ensues as the starlings twist and turn in unison; the starlings nearest the falcon peel away in what look like rippling waves, and the flock takes on the form of a vast black amoeba, twisting and turning across the sky. The falcon's shape is often completely lost amid the shimmering flock. The vast majority of the two million starlings make it through unscathed to roost in trees lining some of the busiest streets in Rome, or in the central square where the underground system terminates and the main bus station is situated.

The influx of so many excited birds to the city centre just as Rome's commuters are heading home creates all sorts of problems. As the starlings arrive and settle down noisily for the night, they produce a constant rain of droppings on commuters, parked cars and pavements, leading to a stream of complaints to the city council.

To counter the starlings' bombardment, teams of people regularly wander the streets with loud hailers, playing hugely amplified recordings of starling alarm calls. The idea is to frighten the birds and drive them away from the street roosts to alternative sites in parks where they cause fewer problems. The alarm calls do, indeed, create panic among the starlings, and great waves of them take to the air as the loud hailers are pointed their way. When the programme first began, the results looked promising. Speakers have also been fixed to some of Rome's great buildings and monuments, and the raucous taped calls screech out automatically at regular intervals. But starlings are intelligent birds, and although they still react to the loud hailers, they seem to have learned that they emit only a false alarm. The overall impression is that they simply move to alternative trees further along the street. Rome may win the battle one day, but for now the lure of the city-centre's warmth is too strong, and the spectacular aerial battles involving the starlings dodging the falcons, together with the street-level ordeals of commuters dodging starling 'rain', continue each night in winter.

NU

centre over the countryside primarily because it is warmer, and the birds burn less energy to keep warm at night. Such city-centre warmth is typical; due to all the heat generated by vehicles, heating systems, lights and reflective tarmac and concrete surfaces, inner-city temperatures are usually a few degrees higher than the surrounding countryside. For starlings, the city is also much safer than the countryside. Apart from the peregrines, there are fewer predators such as martens that might snatch them at a country roost, and no hunters trying to blast them off their perches. So every night vast roosts, some of more than half a million birds, gather in some of the busiest streets and squares in Rome, including the trees above the central bus station. The rain of droppings descending from these roosts creates all sorts of problems for commuters trying to get home as the starlings arrive, and for the city council who have to clean up after them and who are trying to find ways of encouraging the birds to use city parks rather than streets and squares for their roosts (see box, p. 181: 'Starlings in Rome').

Parks have always been an important feature of cities, and great cities like Athens, Madrid and London are famous for the extensive green parks in their centres, many of which date back hundreds of years. Urban life has probably been busy and stressful for its residents ever since the days of rush-hour ancient Rome. In the same way that the public gardens of Rome in the second century AD were no doubt a welcome relief for the citizens of the time, so today's green spaces in cities are also invaluable. For businessmen, commuters, shoppers and visitors, the hustle and bustle of the streets can all become too much after a while. A park, with its open areas, fresher air and slower pace is the perfect place to unwind and relax. Wildlife, too, has always been drawn to such places, sharing them with human visitors. Collections of ornamental ducks often supplement the native pigeons and sparrows, and a visit to a park is never complete for some without stopping to feed the ducks. Quite how important such interaction with wildlife and natural places can be is hard to assess, but appreciation of parks and wildlife is such a universal phenomenon that some believe there is a deep-seated need in us to seek out green spaces and nature generally. For city residents, parks provide the only accessible chance to satisfy this need. City planners seem to have realized this in the past, and created the great parks that survive to this day.

As well as attracting classic urban species such as pigeons and sparrows, which have lived in cities for centuries, more timid creatures from the countryside are increasingly moving into city parks. The Serpentine, a stretch of water which runs through Hyde Park in London, is now home to a few pairs of great-crested grebes. These birds are normally incredibly shy and hard to observe, but can be watched performing their complex courtship routines. These involve rearing up out of the water and paddling furiously with their hind legs, while they shake strips of weed in each other's faces. They also thread their way between the swimmers and boaters on the river, carrying their stripy chicks, while their mate dives for fish to feed tenderly to the chicks.

The urban waterways of London are also home to alien reptiles: red-eared terrapins, which were released after a popular craze for cartoon turtles came to an end. These creatures seem to be doing well in a number of city ponds and lakes, preying on small fish, and surviving the winters by hibernating. American crayfish now live in the Serpentine as well.

Herds of red and fallow deer can be seen in London too, grazing languorously in Richmond Park, overlooked by tall tower blocks. They are the remnants of the herds once kept in this royal hunting park. This mix of species in a city, some with ancient relationships with us, some only recent arrivals from the countryside and others alien introductions, is typical of modern city fauna; the diversity of its origins explains much of its variety. But all city wildlife relies on finding food and space to live, and most requires a tolerant attitude from human residents for it to thrive.

As cities continue to grow and expand, can we assume that city planners will continue to realize the need for green spaces, which both people and wildlife can take advantage of? The answer appears to be yes. There is a growing awareness that, whatever the root cause of the need, people do want green spaces close to where their homes and workplaces are, and choose to live and work where such amenities are provided. The planners also realize that as air pollution becomes a greater and greater problem in cities, parks and other green spaces can help to improve the climate. Trees, grass and other plants capture dust, produce oxygen and raise humidity. So, as cities expand, green areas are being designed into them. Even in the newest and most modern-looking developments such as La Défense, the futuristic business district in Paris, extensive gardens and lawns have been planted for people to wander through. Such green spaces should continue to attract the wildlife of the future as they have done in the past.

Over the last 10,000 years, as human civilization has swept across Europe, wildlife has adapted in all sorts of ways to changed landscapes. The urban habitat represents the most extreme form of change, and the great success that wildlife has had in adapting to city living, and continues to do so, is an encouraging sign for the future. But in the same way that attitudes towards wildlife have been crucial to animal success in cities, so too will our attitudes towards wildlife and wild places be crucial to their survival throughout Europe.

NU

Citizens

LIVING EUROPE

CHAPTER 1:
THE CRADLE
Attenborough, D., *The First Eden* (BBC Books, London, 1987)
Botting, D., *Wild France: Traveller's Guide* (Sheldrake Press, London, 1992)
Finlayson, C., *Birds of the Strait of Gibraltar* (T. & A. D. Poyser Ltd, London, 1992)
Grunfield, F., *Wild Spain* (Sheldrake Press, London, 1988)
Hammond, N., *Artists for Nature in Extremadura* (The Wildlife Art Gallery, Lavenham, 1995)
Hughes, D. J., *Ecology in Ancient Civilisations* (The University of New Mexico Press, Albuquerque, 1975)
Jepson, T., *Wild Italy: Traveller's Guide* (Sheldrake Press, London, 1994)
Kofou, A., *Crete*, (George A.Christopoulos & John C. Bastias, Athens, 1988)
Lever, Sir C., *Naturalized Mammals of the World* (Longman Inc., New York, 1985)
Rackham, O. & Moody, J., *The Making of the Cretan Landscape* (Manchester University Press, 1996)
Raine, P., *Mediterranean Wildlife: The Rough Guide* (Harrap Columbus, Bromley, 1990)

CHAPTER 2:
LAST OF THE WILD WOODS
Duffey, E., *The Forest World* (Orbis Publishing Ltd, London, 1980)
Kuusela, K. F., *Forest Resources in Europe* (Cambridge University Press, 1994)
Peterken, G. F., *Natural Woodland* (Cambridge University Press, 1996)
Walencik, J., *Heartbeat of the Primeval Forest* (Sport I Turystyka – MUZA SA, Warsaw, 1997)
Whitlock, R., *Historic Forests of England* (Moonraker Press, Bradford-on-Avon, 1979)

CHAPTER 3:
FRESH WATER
Field Guide to the Water Life of Britain, (Reader's Digest, London, 1984)
Klosowscy, G. & Stanislaw, I. T., *The Birds of Biebrza's Marshes* (KSAT, Warsaw, 1991)
Shillcock, R. D'Arcy, *Portrait of a Living Marsh* (Inmerc BV, Wormer, The Netherlands, 1993)
Walencik, J., *The Wild River Valley* (Sport I Turystyka – MUZA SA, Warsaw, 1998)

CHAPTER 4:
GRASSLANDS: ANCIENT & MODERN
Aichele, D. & R., and Schwegler, I. I. W. & A., *Wild Flowers of Britain and Europe* (Hamlyn Guide, 1986)
Burton, J. A. & Pearson, B., *Rare Mammals of the World* (Collins, London, 1987)
Gorman, G., *The Birds of Hungary* (Christopher Helm, London, 1996)
Grasslands and Tundra (Time Life Books, Amsterdam, 1985)
Harlan, J. R., *The Living Fields, Our Agricultural Heritage*, Cambridge University Press, 1995)
Hubbard, C. E., *Grasses* (Penguin Books, Harmondsworth, 1954)
Massey Stewart, J., *The Nature of Russia* (Boxtree Ltd, London, 1992)
Smith, B. D., *The Emergence of Agriculture* (Scientific American Library, New York, 1995)
Wilson, R., *The Hedgerow Book* (David & Charles Inc., Newton Abbot, 1979)

CHAPTER 5:
MOUNTAINS & MOORS
Botting, D., *Wilderness Europe* (Time Life Books, Amsterdam, 1976)

Briand, F., Dubost, M., Pitt, D. & Rambaud, D., *The Alps: A System Under Pressure* (IUCN, Chambéry, 1989)
Brooks, B., *British Naturalists' Association Guide to Mountain and Moorland* (The Crowood Press, Marlborough, 1985)
Crowley, K. & Link, M., *Following the Pack: The World of Wolf Research* (Voyageur Press, Inc., Minnesota, 1994)
Darlington, A., *The Natural History of Britain and Northern Europe, Mountains and Moorlands* (Hodder & Stoughton, London, 1978)
Field Guide to the Animals of Britain (Reader's Digest, London, 1984)
Gibbons, B., *A Guide to the National Parks and other Wild Places of Britain and Europe* (New Holland Publishers Ltd, London, 1994)
Grey-Wilson, C. & Blamey, M., *Alpine Flowers* (Collins, London, 1992)
Walker, R., *Walks and Climbs in the Picos de Europa* (Cicerone Press, Milnthorpe, 1993)

CHAPTER 6:
SEA & COAST
Anderson, S., *Seals* (Whittet Books Ltd, London, 1990)
Groombridge, B. *Marine Turtles in the Mediterranean: Distribution, Population Status, Conservation* (Council of Europe, Publishing and Documentation Service, Strasbourg, 1990)
Little, C. & Kitching, J. A., *The Biology of Rocky Shores* (Oxford University Press, 1996)
The Mitchell Beazley Atlas of the Oceans (Mitchell Beazley, London, 1977)
Mojetta, A., *Mediterranean Sea: Guide to the Underwater Life* (Swan Hill Press, Shrewsbury, 1996)
Parker, S.,

Eyewitness Guide: Seashore, Dorling Kindersley Ltd, London, 1989)
Raine, P., *Mediterranean Wildlife: The Rough Guide* (Harrap Columbus, Bromley, 1990)
Viallelle, S., *Dolphins and Whales from the Azores* (Espaco Talassa, Acores, Portugal, 1997)

CHAPTER 7: LAND OF ICE & SNOW
Arlov, T. B., *A Short History of Svalbard* (Norsk Polarinstitutt, Oslo, 1994)
Pielou, E. C., *A Naturalist's Guide to the Arctic* (The University of Chicago Press, 1994)
Umbreit, A., *Guide to Spitsbergen* (Bradt Publications, Bucks., 1991)
Young, S. B., *To the Arctic* (John Wiley & Sons, Inc., New York, 1994)

CHAPTER 8:
CITIZENS
Gilbert, O. L., *The Ecology of Urban Habitats* (Chapman & Hall, London, 1989)
Hohenberg, P. M. & Lees, L. H., *The Making of Urban Europe 1000–1994* (Harvard University Press, Cambridge Mass. and London, 1995)
Hughes, D. J., *Ecology in Ancient Civilisations* (The University of New Mexico Press, Albuquerque, 1975)

GENERAL
Arnold, E. N., Burton, J. A. & Ovenden, D. W., *Collins Field Guide: Reptiles and Amphibians of Britain and Europe* (Collins, London, 1992)
Bartlett, R., *The Making of Europe* (Penguin Books, Harmondsworth, 1993)
Burton, M. H., *Animals of Europe* (Book Club Associates, London, 1979)
Chinery, M., *A Field Guide to the Insects of*

Britain and Northern Europe (Collins, London, 1982)
Cramp, S., Simmons, K. E. L. & Perrins, C. M., *Handbook of the Birds of Europe, The Middle East and North Africa: The Birds of the Western Palearctic, 9 vols* (Oxford University Press, 1984–97)
Europe's Environment: The Dobris Assessment (Earthscan Publications, London, 1995)
Gorman, G., *Where to Watch Birds in Eastern Europe* (Hamlyn, London, 1994)
Hammond, N. & Everett, M., *Birds of Britain and Europe*, Ward Lock, London, 1980)
Heinzel, H., Fitter, R. & Parslow, J., *Collins Pocket Guide: Birds of Britain and Europe with North Africa and the Middle East* (Harper Collins Publishers, London, 1995)
Macdonald, D. & Barrett, P., *Collins Field Guide: Mammals of Britain and Europe* (HarperCollins Publishers, London, 1993)
Macdonald, D., *European Mammals, Evolution and Behaviour* (HarperCollins Publishers, London, 1995)
Morrison, P., *Mammals, Reptiles and Amphibians of Britain and Europe* (Macmillan Publishers, London, 1994)
Pounds, N. J. G., *Historical Geography of Europe* (Cambridge University Press, 1990)
Schama, S., *Landscape and Memory* (HarperCollins Publishers, London, 1995)
Tucker, G. M., & Heath, M. F., *Birds in Europe: Their Conservation Status* (Birdlife International, Cambridge, 1994)
Wirth, Dr H. (ed.) *Nature Reserves in Europe* (Jupiter Books, London, 1981)

As explained in the Acknowledgements, we are hugely indebted to a vast number of people for their help in making the *Living Europe* series. The following lists some of the people who most directly contributed to the experiences and information presented in the book. There were many more that we could have listed if we had unlimited space.

CHAPTER 1: THE CRADLE

Andrea Bonetti; Giorgos Chiras; Antonio Felicioli; Clive Finlayson; Martin Gaethlich; Atanasio Fernandez Garcia; John and Chris Henshall; Tomas Hertzman; Frederic Lamouroux; Petros Lamberakis; Fernando Pulido; Hans Roth; Juan Sanchez-Guzman; Tenuta di San Rossore; Manuela Siefert; Ali Ilhan Tireli; Donald Upton; The Directors and staff of: Abruzzo National Park; Donana National Park; Monfrague Natural Park; Monte Amiata Animal Park.

CHAPTER 2: LAST OF THE WILD WOODS

Jouni Aspi; The Directors and staff of: The Finnish Forest and Park Service; Oulanka Biological Station, Finland; The Polish Academy of Science, Mammals Research Unit in Białowieża, Poland; Ilpo Hanski; Jyrki Makela; Czeslaw Okolow; Jari Peltomaki; Elina Torvinen.

CHAPTER 3: FRESH WATER

Vinko Bartolac; John Colton; the Manager and Fishermen of Dojransko Ezero, Dojran, Macedonia; Graham Drucker; Branko Micevski; Slavko Polak; James and Elena Roberts; The Romanian Ornithological Society; Bozidar Stlinovic; The Directors and staff of: The Ohrid Hydrobiological Institute, Macedonia; The Polish Academy of Science Research Station, Popielno, Poland.

CHAPTER 4: GRASSLANDS: ANCIENT & MODERN

Trevor Ash; Malcolm Brockless; Sue Dewer; Yuri Dukhnich; Elizabeth Dyas; The Game Conservancy Trust, Loddington, England; Gerard Gorman; Chris Haes; Mark Horton-Brown; The Hungarian Ornithological and Nature Conservation Society; Chris Stoate; Professor Varga, Emese Meglecz and Gyorgy Duda; Worldwide Fund for Nature, Austria; The Directors and staff of: The Askania-Nova Reserve, Ukraine; The Hortobágy National Park, Hungary.

CHAPTER 5: MOUNTAINS & MOORS

Dick Balharry; Oscar Sanchez Corral; Teresa Farino; Ovidiu Ionescu and Christoph Promberger; Simone Fluri; Benito Fuertes Marcos; Vittorio Peracino; Francisco Purroy; The Royal Society for the Protection of Birds; Scottish Natural Heritage; Erika Stanciu; Ron Summers; Eric Zimen.

CHAPTER 6: SEA & COAST

Tony Clare; Mike Fedac; Jonathan Gordon; Malcolm Jones; Colin Little; Dan Minchin; Anjelo Mojetta; Kirsi Peck; Alan Rees; Carlos Reis; Chris Reid; Philippe Robert; Javier Romero; Sea Turtle Protection Society of Greece; Tom Walmsley; Vrassidas Zavras.

CHAPTER 7: LAND OF ICE & SNOW

Ian Gjertz; Kit Kovacs; Christian Lydersen; Arne Naevre; Jason Roberts.

CHAPTER 8: CITIZENS

Philiippe Berenger-Levegne; Sue and Dennis Carter; Andrew Crawford; John Coulson; Don Hunford; Malcolm Kerr; Karl Kugelschafter; Guilhelm Lesaffre; Brian Little; Josephine Pithon; Gary Roberts; James Roberts Louise Roberts; Peter and Margaret Smithson.

LIVING EUROPE

Tony Allen: 173; **Nigel Ashcroft:** 145; **Jonathan Clay:** title page, 40 inset, 49, 64 left and right, 68 bottom, 69, 73, 101, 105, 108, 112-113 main picture, 113 inset, 116, 117 main picture, 117 inset; **Vincenzo de Pompeis:** 180; **Piers Finzel:** 37, 160 main picture, 168; **Hardlines:** 8-9, 148; **Ian Hodson:** 140, 141; **Kathryn Jeffs:** 120 inset, 132-133 main picture, 133 inset, 137, 161; **Mags MacRae:** 129; **Oxford Scientific Films/Okapia:** (Martin Wendler) 81; **Oxford Scientific Films/Survival Anglia:** (Konrad Wöthe) 84; **Oxford Scientific Films:** (Barrie E. Watts) 76 main picture, (Ronald Toms) 76 inset, (Richard Packwood) 85 top, (Konrad Wöthe) 85 bottom, 89 left; (Mark Hamblin) 88 right; **Steve Packham:** half title page, 144 inset, 156-157, 157 centre, 157 right; **Rachel Pinnock:** 88 left; 92; **Jason Roberts:** 144 main picture, 152, 153, 156 left; **Nigel Tucker:** 77, 80, 89 right, 93, 96 inset, 97, 100, 104, 109; **Nick Upton:** 12 main picture, 12 inset, 13, 16, 17, 20, 21, 24, 29 left, 29 right, 32 left, 32 right, 33, 36, 120 main picture, 121, 125, 136, 165, 169, 181; **Henrietta Van den Bergh:** 160 inset, 176, 177; **Jan Walencik:** 40 main picture, 41, 44-45, 48, 52, 53, 56, 57, 60 main picture, 60 inset, 61, 65 top and bottom, 68 top, 72, 96 main picture.